IMAGES
of America

KANSAS

IN THE HEART OF TORNADO ALLEY

On May 26, 1917, *The Wichita Eagle* reported, "A twister moved upon the town [of Andale] at 2:25 o'clock. Inhabitants saw the cloud; some thought it appeared 'nasty'; others took little note of it. All at once the town was enveloped in inky darkness; the roar of the twister was like a thousand cataracts among the housetops. Then came 'the explosion,' as they called it. The wrath of the storm had broken. In twenty seconds it was over. Just twenty seconds." (Authors' collection.)

ON THE COVER: A June 1915 storm in Kiowa County created a twister that went between Greensburg and Mullinville. (Courtesy NOAA Photograph Library and Kansas State Historical Society.)

IMAGES
of America

KANSAS

IN THE HEART OF TORNADO ALLEY

Jay M. Price, Craig Torbenson,
Sadonia Corns, Jessica Nellis, and Keith Wondra

ARCADIA
PUBLISHING

ISBN 978-0-7385-7638-1

Published by Arcadia Publishing
Charleston, South Carolina

Printed in the United States of America

Library of Congress Control Number: 2011928645

For all general information, please contact Arcadia Publishing:
Telephone 843-853-2070
Fax 843-853-0044
E-mail sales@arcadiapublishing.com
For customer service and orders:
Toll-Free 1-888-313-2665

Visit us on the Internet at www.arcadiapublishing.com

This book is dedicated to all those who work to better the understanding of tornadoes and who come to the service of their fellow citizens in the wake of tornadic events.

Contents

ACKNOWLEDGMENTS

This project would not have been possible without the help of the National Oceanic and Atmospheric Administration (NOAA), particularly its National Severe Storms Lab (NSSL); National Weather Service (NWS) forecast offices in Dodge City, Goodland, Topeka, and Wichita; the Vortex 2 Project; *The Wichita Eagle*; *Akron (CO) Weekly Pioneer*; *Topeka Capital-Journal*; *Atchison Daily Globe*; *Wellington Daily News*; *Coshocton Daily*; *Emporia Gazette*; *Scientific American*; *Frank Leslie's Illustrated Newspaper*; Kansas State Historical Society; Butler County History Center; Udall Community Historical Museum; Augusta Historical Museum; Frank Walker Museum/Rooks County Historical Society; City of Andover; Kansas Heritage Center; Sisters of St. Joseph, Wichita; River City Brewing Company; Sedgwick County, Kansas, Emergency Management; Sedgwick County Records Management; Topeka Shawnee County Public Library; Kansas Adjutant General's Department; Vornado Fan; Protection Shelters; American Red Cross Midway-Kansas chapter; Kansas Cosmosphere; University of Chicago; Westar Energy, Inc.; 22nd Air Refueling Wing and McConnell Air Force Base; Tinker Air Force Base; Kansas Underground Salt Museum; Underground Vaults and Storage; Library of Congress; KAKE; KFDI; KSN; KWCH; WIBW; Warner Bros. Entertainment, Inc.; Ulrich Museum of Art, Wichita State University; Exploration Place; and Wichita State University Tornado Alley Press Printing Guild. The team wishes to thank Leonard Allen; Thad Allton; Sara Apodaca; Jenna Blum; Keith Brewer; Alan Cook; Lisa Cooley; Brian Corn; Nancy Corns; James Crowder; Dan Dillon; James Dodge; Chuck Doswell; Donna Dreyer; Glen Ediger; Dick Elder; Stan Finger; Daniel Fitzgerald; David Floyd; Thurman Fussell; Duane Graham; Rex Harris; Chance Hayes; Judy Henry; Grant Hewitt; David Hoadley; Andrea Holt; Cheryl Huggins; Greg Johnson; Bethany Kennedy; Bryce Kintigh; Mary Knapp; Raleigh Lackey; Steve Larsen; Susan McCoy; Mallory Medvene; Rachelle Meinecke; Bonar Menninger; Dan Norton; Hal Ottaway; Keith and Jillian Overstake; Marvin and Eudora Petersen; Emily Peterson; George Phillips; Theodore C. Price; Wes Race; Shantel Ringler; Christopher Robrahn; Larry Ruthi; Fred and Lois Satterthwaite; Brett Schauf; Jerry Shaw; Russell Shields; Christen L. Skaer, DVM; Mike Smith; Sue Smith; Dave Strough; Drew Switzer; Dudley Toevs; Cheryl Unruh; Dave Webb; James Williams; Joshua Wurman; and Hong Zhang. Thanks also to all the photographers, named and unnamed, who produced the images found in this book. All quotes without listed sources are taken from author interviews and research.

INTRODUCTION

Every Monday at noon, the sirens sound across Wichita, Kansas. Locals know that as long as it is sunny, the minute-long drone just indicates the regular testing of the city's storm warning system—and lunchtime. If the day is overcast and rainy, the alarm does not sound, ensuring that there is no confusion if real danger is near. However, when weather threatens, the siren prompts people to first head to the television or radio to learn what the situation entails. If danger is close, it is time to seek shelter. Even if there is no immediate threat, there is always the chance that the next several hours will be spent watching warnings scroll across the television screen, with regular shows preempted to feature the latest Doppler images and weather forecasters ready to point out the slightest hint of a "hook echo" on radar. Such is life in "Tornado Alley."

There is nothing inherently Kansan about tornadoes. All states in Tornado Alley—the vast stretch of land in the center of the United States—see their share of truly destructive weather events. Tuscaloosa and Birmingham recently endured two of the most severe twisters in decades, yet few think of Alabama as "the tornado state."

The connection between the tornado and Kansas is as much about image and reputation as hard statistics. To the annoyance of many Kansans, the *Wizard of Oz* has as much to do with this perception as any weather report. Of all the states in Tornado Alley, Kansas seems to be associated with the twister most often, much as Florida is associated with hurricanes, Hawai'i with volcanoes, and California with earthquakes.

It is remarkable how many people assume tornadoes are almost everyday events in Kansas. Kansas's association with destructive weather perhaps keeps some people from moving to the state. Others visit only with a constant, vigilant eye on the sky. Those who live in Kansas know better. There are native-born senior citizens who have never seen so much as a funnel cloud. Most tornadoes are relatively modest and short-lived, touching down in remote areas and causing minimal or isolated damage. Large hail, flooding, and high winds are frequently the most destructive elements of weather in the Sunflower State.

Tornadoes are a part of life in Kansas. Destructive twisters have devastated whole communities, including some that never fully recovered. Yet, there is also a legacy of rebuilding and rebirth, of neighbors and families helping one another. This story includes the many ways that people prepare for severe weather, such as the coordinated efforts of national, state, and local officials along with a host of institutions and private companies, to attempt to bring a level of predictability to the ever-unpredictable nature of storms. In a place where one is never truly out of harm's way, it is perhaps inevitable that those who live in Tornado Alley have found ways to at least harness the image of the twister, if not the winds themselves.

This book explores the relationship between the people of Kansas and the tornado. It is not a comprehensive listing of all major tornadic events in the state; rather, the intention is to show the varied ways in which the tornado has shaped the lives of Kansans—and will likely continue to do so in the future.

This photograph captures a 1914 tornado in El Dorado. An excerpt from a poem/song by Kansas native Shantel Ringler goes, "We are a race of skywatchers who touch Earth and sky at once / The prairie gives nothing up so easily / We are a place to live, to accept a dare / Where loneliness and isolation are dominated by badlands / Where well-worn pews and illusions of wagon tracks in motion unearth shadows of wild soldiers and riders of Gods / Where sunflowers stalk snowdrifts / Where yucca and sagebrush, sassafras and sumac stretch from Cedar Vale to Sin City." (Courtesy Butler County History Center.)

One

Tornado Alley

The central part of the United States and Canada is part of a vast lowland region extending some 1,200 miles east to west, from the Rockies to the Appalachians, and 2,500 miles north to south, from the Gulf of Mexico to the Arctic Ocean. The topography is important because it helps to explain why tornadoes are so common here. With no significant physical barriers impeding airflow, this part of the continent is the world's most active tornado region and has some of its most violent weather. This frequency of tornadoes led Jennifer Wiley to dub the area "Tornado Alley" in 1904.

Four ingredients provide the right mixture for the creation of tornadoes in this area. The first is a strong high-altitude jet stream that bends far to the south and generates unstable atmospheric conditions. The remaining three are air masses that have their own unique characteristics: to the north is cold, dry air that blows from Canada; to the southwest is warm, dry air; and to the south is warm, moist air coming up from the Gulf of Mexico. These four elements combine to produce intense storms and can result in a tornado. Even under these conditions, tornadoes only form about 10 percent of severe storms. The exact ingredients that tip the balance in favor of a particular scenario producing a tornado remain a mystery.

While the boundaries of Tornado Alley are debatable, there is widespread agreement that the states of Oklahoma, Kansas, Nebraska, and much of Texas form the core of the alley. Between 2000 and 2010, these four states experienced 3,908 tornadoes, with 40 percent occurring in Texas and 31 percent in Kansas. Other places identified as part of the alley have included the western parts of Missouri and Iowa and the southern parts of South Dakota and Minnesota.

Several states, including Alabama, Florida, Missouri, and Illinois, are also noted for their tornadoes. As a result, some researchers have identified two smaller geographic areas where tornadoes occur. "Dixie Alley" swings through Arkansas, Louisiana, Mississippi, Alabama, and parts of Georgia and Tennessee, while "Hoosier Alley" includes Illinois, Indiana, southern Michigan, and western Ohio. Despite the names, neither can compare with the sheer number of tornadoes in Tornado Alley—or the legacy.

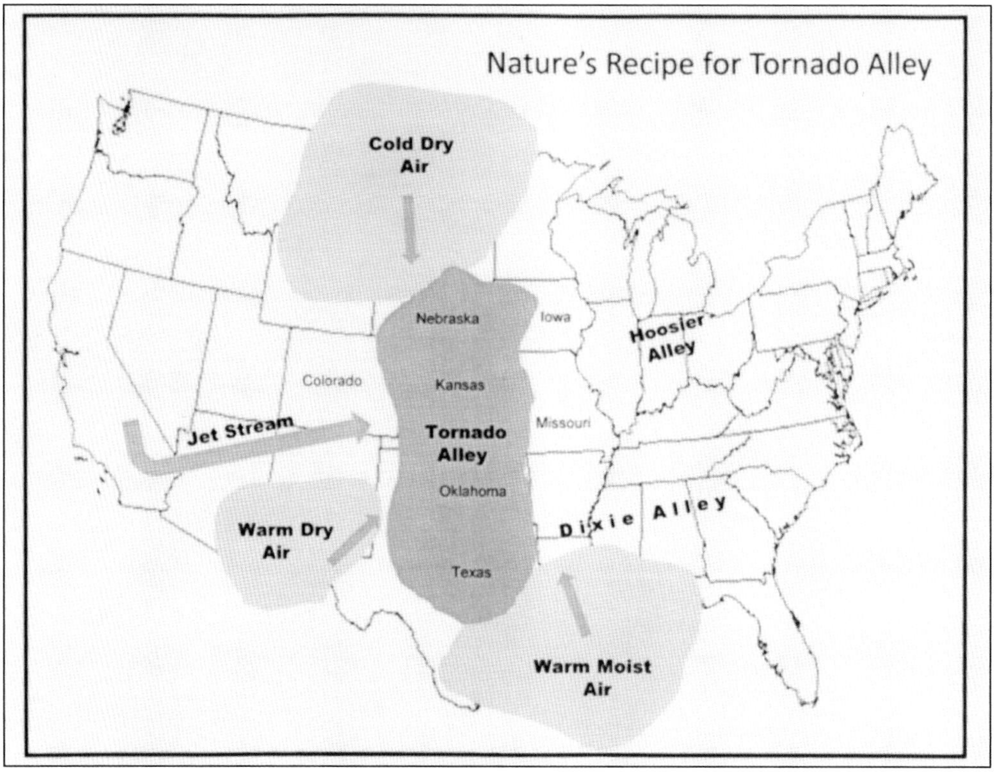

Four ingredients help to create Tornado Alley: a strong jet stream; cold, dry air coming from Canada; warm, dry air coming from the southwest; and warm, moist air coming from the Gulf of Mexico. When these four ingredients come together, the result may produce a tornado—hence the term "Tornado Alley." (Courtesy Craig Torbenson; adapted from NOAA maps.)

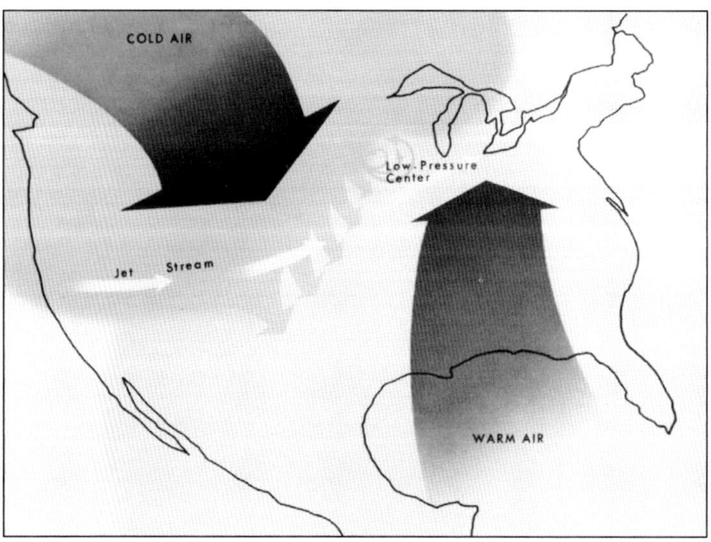

For the rest of the United States, the creation of tornadoes is more dependent on cold air from the north and warm air from the Gulf of Mexico. When these two fronts meet, the result can be violent weather, although strong upper winds are still needed. This image is from the 1966 Environmental Science Services Administration booklet entitled "Tornadoes." (Courtesy NOAA.)

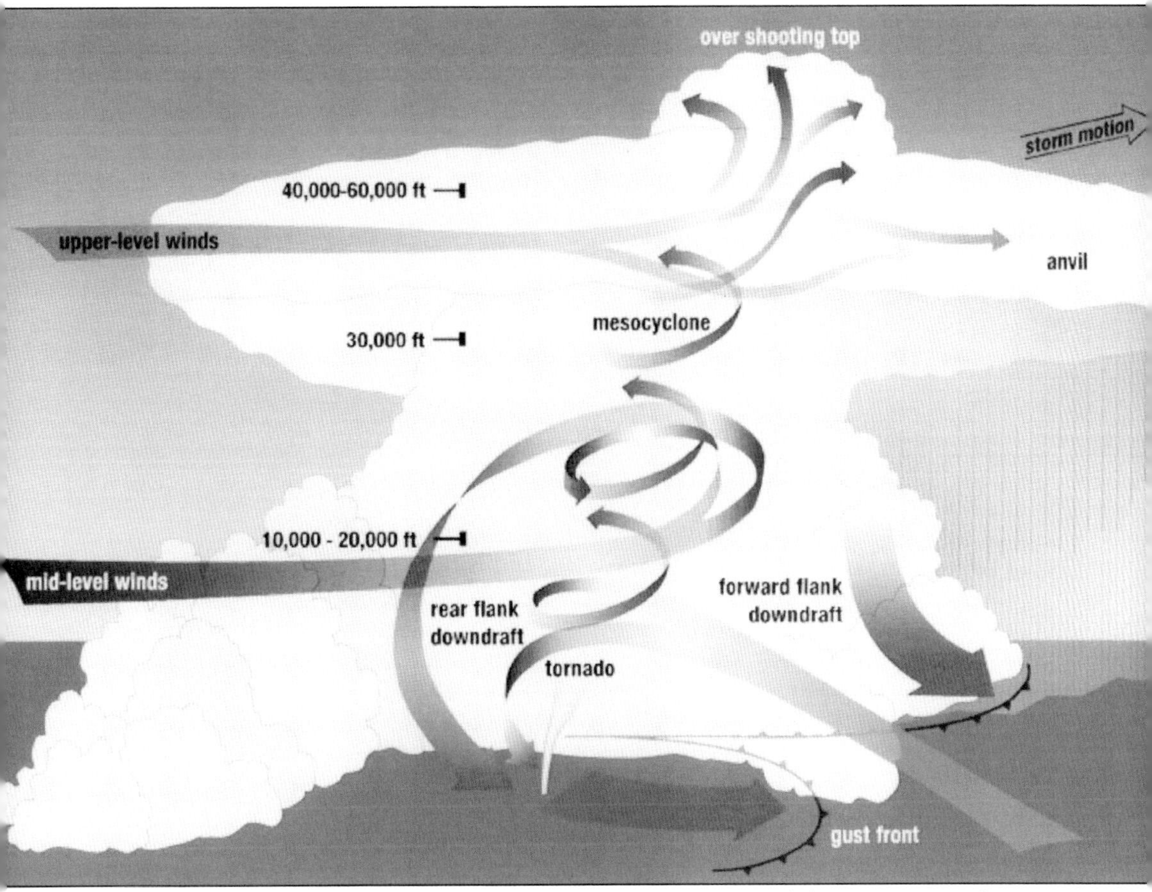

It is from the supercell thunderstorm that most of the strongest and dangerous tornadoes are spawned. These storms begin with an updraft of warm, moist air that can extend up to 10 miles in the atmosphere. When this updraft begins, it creates a mesocyclone, which causes the supercell to rotate. The next ingredient for a tornado is a strong current of cool air moving downward on the backside of the storm called the rear flank downdraft. Since this air is colder it sinks, and as it increases in speed (up to 100 miles an hour) a tornado forms between the warm updraft and the cool downdraft. The result is a tornado dipping out of the base of the storm, or its wall cloud. Super-cell storms can be small or large and can last up to several hours and may spawn multiple tornadoes. (Courtesy NOAA Photograph Library, NOAA's National Severe Storms Laboratory [NSSL] Collection.)

"Stormy skies interrupt peaceful April days in Kansas, and we were sitting six miles southeast of Marion, Kansas, in Marion County that day [April 3, 2011]. The storms were located over Junction City. Note the mammatus clouds [pouch-shaped formations] and the anvil shape of the thunderstorm. The more mammatus clouds that appear, the more severe the storm," recalled local photographer Brett Schauf, on a storm chasing event. (Courtesy Brett Schauf.)

As a storm moves across the land, the trailing edge may experience rotation. If rotation continues, a bowl-like wall cloud may form, which may produce a rotating funnel cloud. If the funnel touches the ground, it becomes a tornado. Brett Schauf describes this scene, "Here, a wall cloud drifts across ripening Kansas wheat fields. We were sitting seven miles south of Hanston, Kansas, in Hodgeman County." (Courtesy Brett Schauf.)

In this image from May 22, 2011, ominous clouds near Chetopa, Kansas, are just starting to show rotation. This storm system devastated Joplin, Missouri, later that evening. (Courtesy Bryce Kintigh.)

Tornadoes usually form toward the rear of a moving storm, southwest of the main area of rainfall. Not all tornadoes are this visible, however. A rain-wrapped tornado can be hidden from view, and even a trained observer might not know how dangerous the situation is until it is too late. As Mike Smith, the CEO and founder of WeatherData, warns, "The thought that amateurs can chase tornadoes is extremely dangerous." (Courtesy Bryce Kintigh.)

Technically, any rotating weather system is a "cyclone." Tornadoes are one form; hurricanes are cyclones, too, but on a larger scale. Therefore, all tornadoes are cyclones, but not all cyclones are tornadoes. Although large tornadoes get the headlines, most are relatively modest, such as the one at left, in Ellis, Kansas, or the one below, from Lebanon, Kansas. Both images appeared in the 1919 edition of *Monthly Weather Review.* (Courtesy NOAA.)

Sometimes called the father of modern storm chasing, David Hoadley, noted, "I can't recall ever hearing it [the term 'twister'] used by storm chasers. This may be a combination of several things. First, in the age of abbreviated computer-speak, single and trendy syllables are preferred, such as 'tube,' 'cone,' or 'wedge.' For some dramatic or large tornadoes, sometimes 'elephant trunk' or 'stovepipe.' Many who want to sound sophisticated probably consider 'twister' as quaint and dated." (Courtesy NOAA.)

Sometimes, what looks like a threat is really what some at the National Weather Service office in Wichita refer to as an "SLC," or "Scary Looking Cloud." Knowing the difference between an SLC and real danger, however, takes training and practice. Even experienced weather spotters can interpret the signs incorrectly. (At right, courtesy Philip Nellis; below, Keith Wondra.)

In contrast to tornadoes, which take place in a relatively quick time frame and leave a relatively confined footprint, floods can cover larger areas and submerge locations for extended periods. It can take far longer for a community to come back from a flood than from even a strong tornado. (Courtesy Augusta Historical Society.)

The most famous flood in Kansas's recent history occurred in 1951. Record rainfall in May, June, and July led to record flooding. Some 150 communities in Kansas and Missouri, including Augusta, Kansas (seen here), experienced a total of nearly $1 billion in damages. (Courtesy Augusta Historical Society.)

Recalling his own hail experience, Wichita State University Geographer Craig Torbenson recalled, "Around six in the morning it started to rain and hail. After a few minutes it stopped and with a roar the house shook for a few seconds. By the time I jumped out of bed it was over. Behind our house ran electrical lines on double wooden posts. Six posts came down from these winds." This image depicts the damage of straight-line winds from a much earlier event. (Courtesy Westar Energy, Inc.)

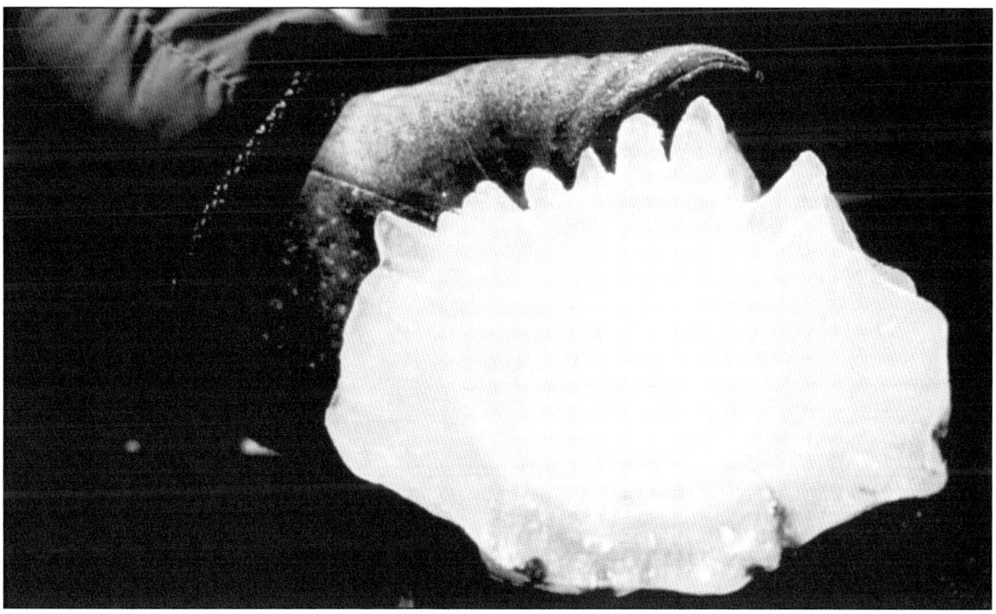

Hail is one of the most damaging consequences of severe weather on the Great Plains, sometimes dubbed "Hail Alley." As a ball of ice drops, sometimes it falls into a strong updraft and rises into the cooler air at the top of the storm. Each time this happens, a new layer of ice forms on the hailstone, as seen in this cross-section of one. (Courtesy NOAA Photograph Library, NOAA's NSSL Collection.)

Among Native Americans, the tornado could symbolize creativity and power or destruction and danger depending on the tribe. The Lakota believe that Yumni, the whirlwind, lives with his brother, the south wind. Often depicted as a cocoon, the whirlwind's unstoppable power is a symbol of warrior strength. Whirlwind Soldier, shown here representing the Rosebud Reservation in 1925, may have a cocoon attached to the left shoulder of his shirt. (Courtesy Library of Congress.)

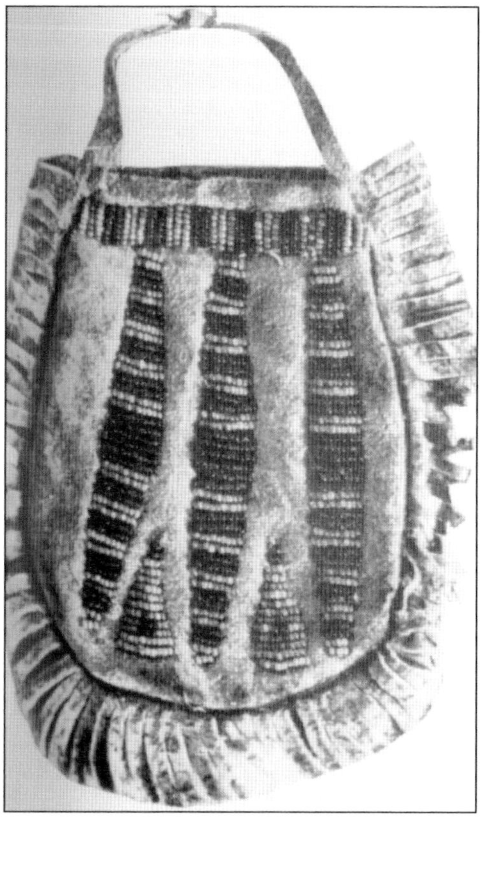

American anthropologist Clark Wissler recalled, "The three upright figures [on this Lakota bag] are said to represent the whirlwind. The cause of the whirlwind is said to emanate from the power of the moth, the chrysalis of which is represented in the conventional design." This image is from the 1904 *Bulletin of the American Museum of Natural History*. (Courtesy American Museum of Natural History.)

For the Arapaho, the tornado is a more a source of creation associated with the first woman, Whirlwind Woman, whose wanderings at the world's creation are the inspiration for this design. This image is from the 1902 *Bulletin of the American Museum of Natural History*. (Courtesy American Museum of Natural History.)

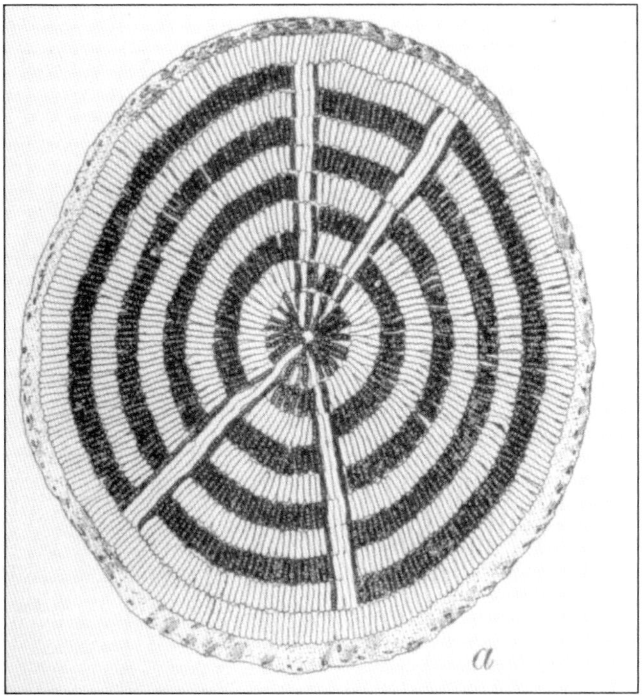

When asked about tornado imagery among the Osage, Jerry Shaw, assistant instructor of minority studies and active member of the Osage tribe, remembered, "My folks taught that whirlwinds had evil in them and that one should stay out of the line of winds. Mother was always very strict about getting the children out of the way of the wind." (Courtesy Topeka Shawnee County Public Library.)

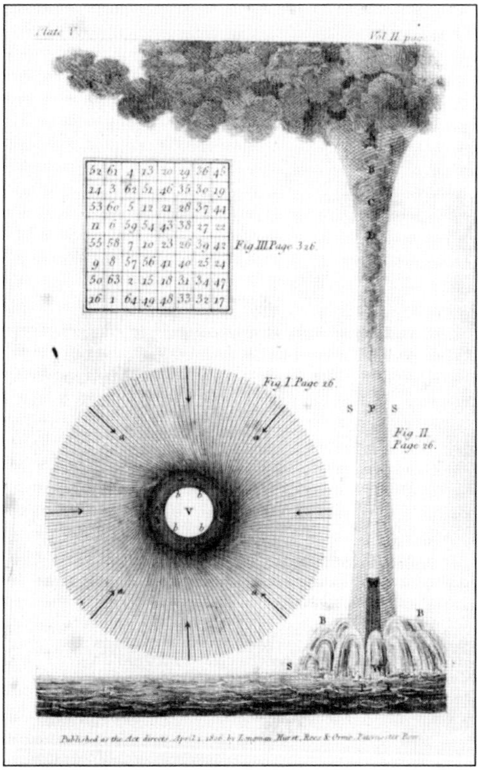

Tornadoes and their aquatic counterparts, waterspouts, have inspired both terror and curiosity. Benjamin Franklin, for example, attempted to study these vortices. This image is from Franklin's paper entitled "Waterspouts and Whirlwinds," republished in the 1806 work *The Complete Works in Philosophy, Politics, and Morals of the Late Dr. Benjamin Franklin*. (Courtesy NOAA.)

In the 19th century, when glass-plate cameras required subjects to stay still for long exposure times, tornadoes were very difficult to photograph. This 1884 image from South Dakota is among the oldest known tornado photographs. (Courtesy NOAA.)

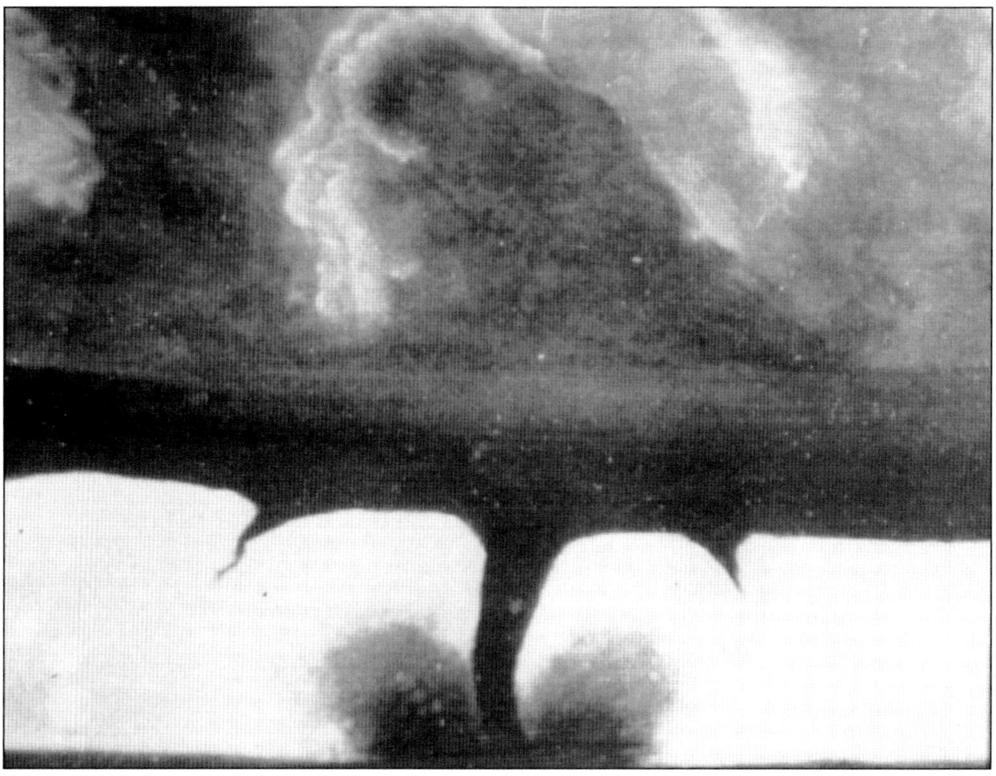

Tetsuya "Theodore" Fujita, while at the University of Chicago, became famous for measuring tornado intensity. The Fujita scale, launched in the 1970s, classified tornadoes on a scale from zero to five based on the amount of damage in the twister's wake. In 2006, NOAA announced an "Enhanced Fujita" (or "EF") scale based on more precise criteria. The first reported EF5 tornado occurred in Greensburg, Kansas, in 2007. (Courtesy University of Chicago.)

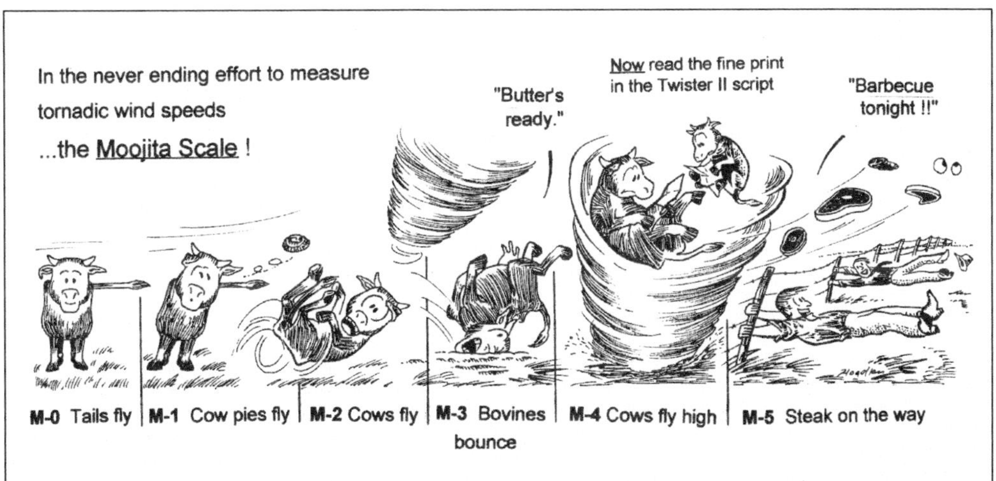

Weather spotting has a tendency to spawn dark humor. Many tornadoes have struck amidst herds of cows, resulting in several versions of a mock "Moojita" scale. (Courtesy David Hoadley.)

Even with improvements in technology, there is plenty that scientists do not know about tornadoes. In 2009, several institutions, including the Center for Severe Weather Research, the National Severe Storms Laboratory, the University of Oklahoma, the University of Massachusetts, the Office of Naval Research, and Texas Tech, united in a two-year effort called Vortex 2 to study and track tornadoes across the Great Plains. (Courtesy Gino deGrandis, Center for Severe Weather Research.)

The Vortex 2 project, directed by Joshua Wurman (pictured) from the Center for Severe Weather Research, involved over 100 scientists and crew members traveling in 50 vehicles. (Courtesy Herb Stein, Center for Severe Weather Research.)

The closer a Doppler radar is to a storm, the more detailed and accurate the readings; therefore, the Vortex 2 project made heavy use of "Doppler on Wheels" (DOW) trucks. Teams in mobile units dropped small "tornado pods" of sensors in front of storms to gather more information. (Above, courtesy Herb Stein, Center for Severe Weather Research; below, Gino deGrandis, Center for Severe Weather Research.)

Radar is an invaluable tool, but it works best for nearby weather events as it loses resolution the farther away a storm system occurs. The best data comes from instruments close to tornadic storms. Scientists have attempted to place objects in the path of tornadoes to capture data. Instruments such as this "TOtable Tornado Observatory" (TOTO) had promise but were difficult to position properly. (Courtesy NOAA Photograph Library, NOAA's NSSL Collection.)

Modeled on the TOTO concept, the "Dorothy II" device appeared in the 1996 Warner Brothers movie *Twister*, a film that helped popularize storm chasing. This prop now resides in Underground Vaults and Storage, 650 feet below the surface of Hutchinson, Kansas. Created in 1959 in a former salt mine, Underground Vaults and Storage houses a number of movie artifacts, including the original reels of *The Wizard of Oz*. (Photograph by Jay M. Price, courtesy Warner Bros. Entertainment, Inc. and Underground Vaults and Storage, Inc.)

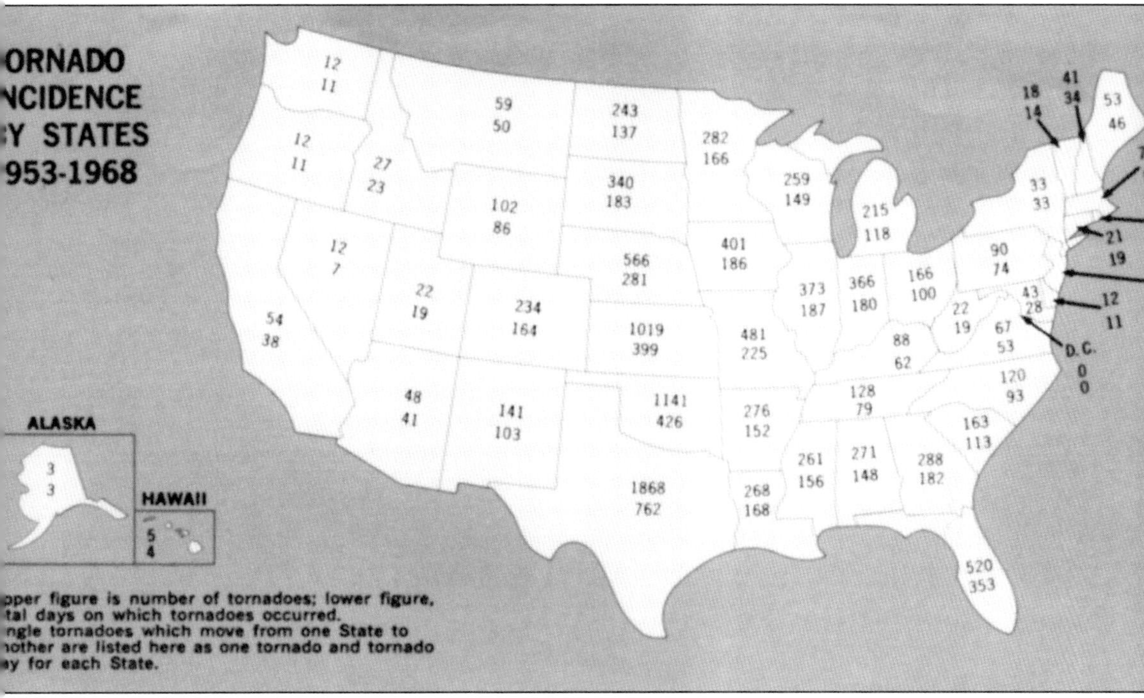

All of the continental United States can experience tornadoes, as shown on this map from 1968. Oklahoma and Texas actually endured more tornadoes than Kansas in the 1950s and 1960s, even though these were the years of the Udall, El Dorado, and Topeka events. On the Great Plains, twisters tend to occur in spring and summer, while in Dixie Alley tornadic storms (not counting those associated with hurricanes) often occur in late winter and early spring. This image is from the U.S. Weather Bureau's *Severe Local Storm Warning Service and Tornado Statistics, 1953–1968.* (Courtesy NOAA.)

People remember images such as this one long after the fact, adding color to the stories they tell when explaining the freakiness of nature. This image of a phonograph record blown into a crack in a utility pole was taken in Ada, Oklahoma, on April 20, 1973. (Courtesy NOAA.)

Noted DOW inventor and atmospheric scientist Joshua Wurman commented, "It's not the winds that hurt. It's the bricks in the wind." Even a mailbox can be a projectile, as this image from the 1965 Palm Sunday tornado in Michigan attests. (Courtesy Theodore C. Price.)

Because of the high velocity associated with tornadic winds, items like this spoon can become embedded into materials that would otherwise not give way. (Courtesy Duane Graham.)

Benjamin Franklin, in a letter to John Perkins on February 4, 1753, wrote, "By its Force it tears Buildings to Pieces, twists up great Trees by the Roots, &c. and by its spiral Motion raises the Fragments . . . [that] fly off in Tangent Lines as Stones out of a Sling, and fall on all Sides and at great Distances." (Courtesy Grant Hewitt.)

Although Kansas and the Great Plains rest in the heart of Tornado Alley, devastating tornadoes take place across the country. The spring of 2011 was one of the most devastating tornado seasons in recent memory, with twisters striking from Tuscaloosa, Alabama, to Springfield, Massachusetts. The community of Joplin, Missouri, was one of the worst hit. Storm chaser Bryce Kintigh was in the area at the time and took these photographs of the ruins of an Academy Sports+Outdoors store and a filling station literally minutes after the tornado had passed. (Both, courtesy Bryce Kintigh.)

Tornadoes and other disasters tend to bring out the willingness of people to assist others. Here, relief workers are ready to help after the storm in Joplin, Missouri. (Courtesy Emilie Petersen.)

The tornado season of spring 2011 brought a shift of notable activity to Dixie Alley, often resulting in higher casualties due to a number of factors. In some places, high water tables make basements impractical. In Joplin, as in many areas, residents had grown complacent to hearing sirens sound, not fully realizing the danger that was looming. (Courtesy Emilie Petersen.)

A.A. Adams captured this image of a tornado in Anderson County in 1884. It is one of the earliest photographs of a twister ever taken in Kansas. (Courtesy Kansas State Historical Society.)

Two

"The Sky Just Didn't Look Right"

The story of tornadoes in Kansas is an ongoing clash between perception and reality. For example, most tornadoes in Kansas occur in the state's wide-open spaces, far away from population centers; however, the most memorable ones are those that devastated settled areas. People outside of Kansas may assume that tornadoes are daily happenings, with graphic descriptions of events in places like Irving seeming to confirm the "Cyclone State" image.

Kansans themselves can hold on to certain myths and beliefs about tornado behavior, even in the face of case studies to the contrary. One myth states that tornadoes never strike at the confluence of two rivers, but being at confluences did not spare residents in the vicinities of Emporia, Augusta, Douglass, Arkansas City, and Wichita.

Another popular myth is that tornadoes do not cross hills. For over a century, Topekans took comfort in the belief that Burnett's Mound would protect the city from tornadoes. They were proven wrong when an F5 tore through the city on June 8, 1966.

Some believed that tornadoes do not strike at night due to the absence of heat from the sun, a myth shattered on May 25, 1955, when Kansas's deadliest tornado struck Udall at 10:30 p.m., killing 77 people. More recently, a tornado struck Hoisington after sunset in 2001.

The most well-known tornado myth states that tornadoes do not strike the same place more than once—a fallacy that endures despite the stories of Greensburg, Udall, Haysville, and Wichita, which have all endured multiple tornado events. Codell, Kansas, which was hit on May 20 three years in a row (1916–1918), provides an especially vivid example.

One tornado reality is endurance. No sooner had a tornado left its mark than a farmer bought new equipment and planted crops for the next season, a community started rebuilding, and people began to put shattered lives back in order. Rebuilding and starting anew is also part of the Kansas story; one that, unlike the myths, is apparent in multiple examples. In some places, the scars from tornadic events remain on both the landscape and with the people. In other cases, the rebuilding is so successful that memories of a particularly fateful day are forgotten even among locals.

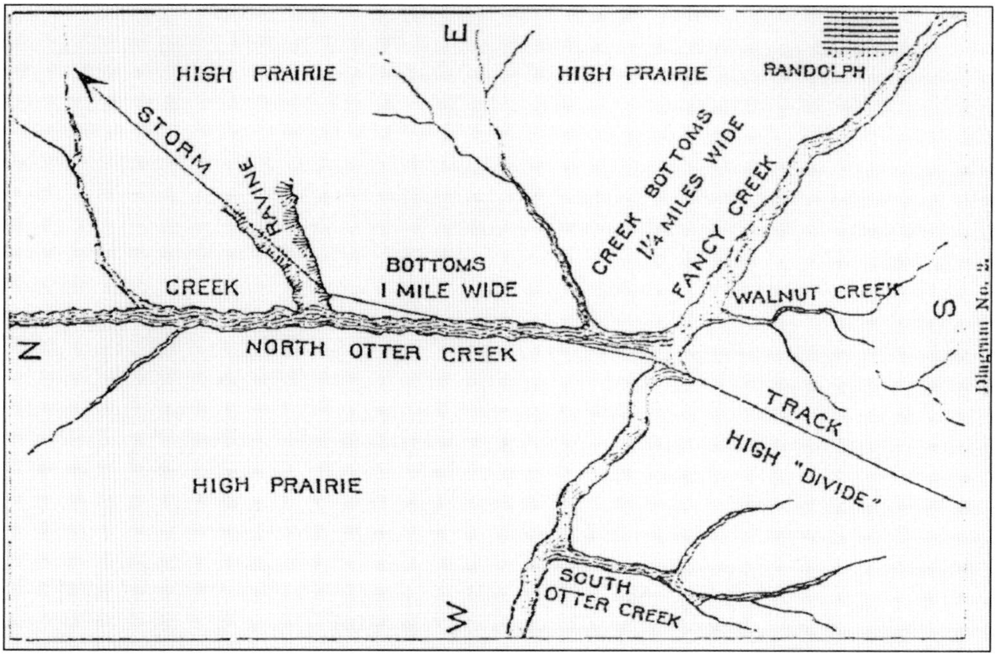

On May 30, 1879, Marshall County—in particular, the town of Irving—suffered not one, but two especially vicious tornadoes; the second perhaps over a mile and a half wide. The communities affected were relatively small in population, but the gruesome deaths (including that of a woman named Dorothy Gale) and the horrific injuries of residents attracted national attention. John P. Finley of the US Signal Corps came out to investigate, and the storms appeared in an article in *Scientific American*. Modern writers credit the Irving twisters as the root of Kansas's tornadic reputation. These images are from Finley's "Report of the Tornadoes of May 29 and 30, 1879, in Kansas, Nebraska, Missouri, and Iowa." (Courtesy US Army Signal Corps.)

Nineteenth-century portrayals of tornadoes featured dramatic scenes of people cowering before sinister vortices. Notice that the funnel, wider toward the base, seems to be upside down in this image. (Courtesy *Scientific American*.)

The April 22, 1882, *Frank Leslie's Illustrated Newspaper* reported, "In Rice County, Kansas, on the night of the 6th [April, 1882], a cyclone demolished twenty out of twenty-six buildings in the town of Chase, and did other damage. It was accompanied by a veritable waterspout, pouring a deluge of water in some places and drowning everything loose in other spots. The wind was so violent that it sucked all of the water out of the wells." (Courtesy *Frank Leslie's Illustrated Newspaper*.)

On April 5, 1882, the citizens of Stafford County were voting for a permanent county seat when a cyclone struck the polling place in Stafford. Part of the ballot box survived (and now resides at the Kansas State Historical Society), but the contents did not. In a special follow-up election, St. John won the vote for county seat, much to the chagrin of the residents of Stafford. (Courtesy Jay M. Price.)

The destruction, virtually, of Fort Riley by the recent cyclone that visited Western Kansas, is reported, and already the question is agitated whether it will pay the government to reconstruct it, or whether it would be cheaper to abandon it. As the fort has been used as a depot for cavalry supplies and winter quarters for that arm of the service, for years, it is too profitable a concern for Western Kansas to see it abandoned, and there will be political influence enough used to maintain it as long as corn is raised and hay mowed in the valleys of the Republican and Smoky Hill.

The year of 1882 seems to have been a particularly vicious one for severe weather, as shown in this article from the April 12, 1882, edition of the *Atchison Globe*. (Courtesy *Atchison Globe*.)

The June 8, 1906, *Coshocton Daily Age* reported, "The town was practically destroyed. About 80 persons were injured. The most seriously hurt are: Katie Fendrichs, 12, leg broken; Henry Ratzlaff, a farmer, hurt internally, may die; Dr. Peter Richert, injured about head; Rev. John Toevs, leg broken. The tornado laid waste a strip 200 yards wide. Several stores and 12 residences were demolished, and every residence in town was damaged." (Authors' collection.)

An excerpt from *The Annals of Kansas, Vol. 1*, by the Kansas State Historical Society, states, "The great floods of 1903 were reaching their crest. They had been preceded by nearly a month of continuous rain, frequently accompanied by hail and tornadoes . . . Kansas became 'a raging wasteland from bluff to bluff.' " This image depicts tornado damage from the same stormy year. (Courtesy Augusta Historical Society.)

A 1909 twister devastated the community of Red Bud, a few miles north of Udall, long before the area's infamous 1955 tornado. (Courtesy Keith Brewer.)

The back of this postcard reads, "Here is some more of the work of the cyclone. We had another frost last night but no rain yet it is so very dry. Have had lettuce, radishes and onions from my own garden." (Courtesy Hal Ottaway.)

In *Flyover People*, author Cheryl Unruh writes, "As for living with the threat of tornadoes, that's just part of being a Kansan. We take the black funnels in stride. There's a certain amount of pride and bravado that comes from living on this land where danger hangs in the air." These images of a funnel cloud in Minneapolis, Kansas (at right), and tornado in Solomon, Kansas (below), appeared in the 1919 *Monthly Weather Review*. (Both, courtesy NOAA.)

FIG. 2.—Tornado cloud at Solomon, Kans.

The town of Codell, Kansas, was hit by a tornado on the same day, May 20, for three consecutive years—in 1916, 1917, and 1918. This unique occurrence made it into *Ripley's Believe It or Not!* The first tornado was just west of town while the second was just east of town. The 1916 and 1917 storms did not result in any casualties. (Both, courtesy Frank Walker Museum/Rooks County Historical Society.)

The third tornado, which hit in 1918, went right through Codell and wiped out most of the residential area, much of the downtown business district, both churches, and the school. It also killed 10 people in and around Codell. The town never fully recovered after this disaster. (Courtesy Frank Walker Museum/Rooks County Historical Society.)

On May 26, 1917, *The Wichita Eagle* reported, "The tornado which destroyed half of Andale, barely missed Sedgwick and laid Auline to waste, sped along on the Kansas plains for fully eighty miles, destroying everything in its path. It probably was the most deadly and destructive twister that ever visited Kansas." Among the casualties were 26 humans, as well as animals such as this horse. (Authors' collection.)

When a tornado came through Halstead in 1910, it demolished the Jones Building (seen here). On the back of the postcard, the writer curiously discusses only ordinary details of family life and makes no mention whatsoever of the disaster. (Courtesy Grant Hewitt.)

The back of this postcard reads, "How does this look to you? They are getting ready to build again. Will have it done so we can harvest I guess." (Courtesy Grant Hewitt.)

While most tornadoes in Kansas strike in spring and summer, the town of Zyba, in the far north of Cowley County, endured a twister in November 1915. *The Wichita Eagle* reported the event with the headline "Zyba Wiped Off the Map." (Authors' collection.)

"When I came to I was standing . . . in a cold and pouring rain wearing only a nightgown. . . . They flagged down the next train and put us in the baggage car and brought us to Wichita to the hospital. My mother had a crushed chest and a punctured lung and died very shortly. My Dad had a broken shoulder and internal injuries but he lived," recounted Mary Gordon. (Authors' collection.)

Some places have had multiple tornado experiences, debunking the myth that tornadoes never strike the same area twice. This storm in Kiowa County in June 1915 created a twister that went between Greensburg and Mullinville. (Courtesy NOAA Photograph Library and Kansas State Historical Society.)

The June 1, 1923, *Akron (CO) Weekly Pioneer* reported, "One person was near death, more than a score were suffering from injuries and more than 100 were homeless as the result of a tornado which struck Greensburg [seen above and below]. Damage was estimated at $150,000. The tornado, which swept from the southeast to the northwest thru the outskirts of the town, destroyed seventeen houses and damaged more than a score of others." (Both, courtesy Grant Hewitt.)

The July 11, 1924, *Wichita Eagle* stated, "The city of Augusta, Kansas, was struck by both a cyclone and a tornado. While a gale of cyclonic nature was blowing from the north a tornado struck the west edge of the city and then swept through the main part of the town, demolishing the stone Catholic church and wrecking practically every business building on State street, the main street of the place." This scene captures the damage from the storm. (Courtesy Augusta Historical Society.)

The 1924 Augusta tornado damaged the top two floors of the five-story Moyle apartment building, the community's tallest structure. The building still stands, but now it has three stories instead of five. (Courtesy Augusta Historical Society.)

Augusta resident William Warner had recently purchased a car and parked in a garage. The storm picked up the garage and carried it a block down the street, depositing it in a pile of rubble. Post-storm inspection showed the car was still standing on the garage floor—without a scratch. However, the owner of this vehicle was not so lucky. (Courtesy Augusta Historical Society.)

This picture shows the downed Dodge Brothers sign on State Street. Some 16 structures were heavily damaged, including the newly constructed high school, lumberyard, and newspaper building. Several injuries occurred in a lunchroom where people were gathered. The hospital was right in the tornado's path, but the cyclone lifted to miss the structure before coming down and demolishing the building just a few feet away. (Courtesy Augusta Historical Society.)

Despite the immediate danger, curiosity brings people outside to gawk at tornadoes. Here, residents of Augusta halt their daily tasks to view a tornado roaring by. At the time, before there were coordinated warning systems, direct observation was one of the few ways people knew they were in danger. This dangerous practice has been rendered unnecessary by present-day warning technology. (Courtesy Augusta Historical Society.)

Violent winds were more than just curiosities for oil-field workers who had to clean up wrecked derricks, as shown in these photographs of a toppled rig in the 1920s. (At right, courtesy Butler County History Center; below, Augusta Historical Society.)

KANSAS' GREATEST NEWSPAPER—LARGEST PAID CIRCULATION IN KANSAS

THE DAY IS PAST when news was spread only by word of mouth. Read your Wichita Beacon for today's news today

THE WICHITA BEACON

WHEN YOU WANT results you use Beacon want ads which bring returns quickly and inexpensively. Just phone 3-2211.

THE BEACON IS THE ONLY EVENING NEWSPAPER IN WICHITA RECEIVING ASSOCIATED PRESS NEWS DISPATCHES

VOL. 83, NO. 125 — WICHITA, KANSAS, MONDAY, FEBRUARY 25, 1935 — Phone Dial 3-2211 — REGULAR EDITION — 14 PAGES

4 DEAD, 130 INJURED IN TORNADO

Six Hurt, Damage Reaches Thousands Here

FIVE-CENT BUS FARE STARTS IN WICHITA TODAY

Nickel Ride Returns to City After Absence of 15 Years

It's here again—the five-cent ride!

After an absence of 15 years the lowly nickel came back to Wichita Monday morning as a welcome medium of transportation.

WHEN TORNADO WAS MOWING PATH THRU RIVER-BOTTOM WOODS

This remarkable close-up view of Sunday's tornado was taken by Robert H. Richards of The Beacon staff as the swirling funnel-shaped wind cloud shortly after 2 p. m. Sunday cut a path thru the Arkansas River bottoms northwest of Wichita demolishing farm homes and barns and uprooting great cottonwood trees as it traveled to the northeast thru suburban Wichita. This photograph is from an unretouched negative just as it came from the camera, showing in all natural detail the action of the tornado. (Photograph Copyright 1935, Wichita Beacon.)

MANY ESCAPES FROM DEATH ARE RECOUNTED

Houses Demolished and Trees Uprooted at Wichita Heights

Six persons were injured and property damage ran into thousands of dollars when a tornado swept out of the west Sunday afternoon to strike suburban residences and level Wichita Heights, suburb north of the city.

STORM FREAKS

STORM STRIKES THREE STATES IN MIDDLEWEST

Homes Are Destroyed; Twister Hits Kansas, Missouri, Oklahoma

Kansas City, Feb. —Blizzards, tornado, dust storms — a weather mixture — marked their passage with death the Midwest today.

STORM COSTS $100,000 AT INDEPENDENCE

Today

Mrs. Roosevelt's Fear
Blonde Mountain Beauty
One Glance Killed
Planes Forbidden

Indian Tornado Legend Proven Again in Wichita

Redman Said Rivers Will Keep Twisters From City

Seven Houses Destroyed as Tornado Sweeps Over City

Independence, Kas., Feb. 25.—Conservative estimates of the damage wrought by a tornado which struck here at 5:10 p. m. Sunday were placed at $100,000 this morning. Seven houses were completely demolished, 14 partially wrecked and a score of others damaged.

ONE IS KILLED IN MINING TOWN

BEACON MAN PHOTOGRAPHS STORM

Market Quotations

Grabs His Camera and Snaps Tornado Scenes From Home

Oil Editor Right on Job as Twister Sweeps by Home in Suburbs

By ROBERT H. RICHARDS

I have lived in Kansas practically all my life but yesterday was the only time I ever saw a tornado from a front row seat. It wasn't exactly a front row seat for I was out in my orchard at Gilder's Court, at the northwest edge of Wichita.

Dust Buries Snow at Dodge City

The Weather

Will Rogers Wires:

Letters Bare Love of Girls For Fliers

American Sisters Declare "Exception Has Been Made for Us" in Notes to Parents

Walter Winchell On Broadway

Biographies That Haven't Been Written

Ellis White, of Laguna, Calif., several years ago invented the "Jazzbird," an impish device for insuring a Bronx cheer thru the exhaust of an automobile. Ellis cleaned up a fortune on the "Jazzbird" and put the

Mercury Toboggans To 13 Above Here

A 51-degree drop in temperature in a period of hours was recorded as Wichita experienced winter following rain and hail which turned to snow after midnight.

The drought of the Dust Bowl in the 1930s meant that there was less moisture to form major storms, including those that could spawn tornadoes. However, tornadoes still occurred, including the one pictured here, which struck Park City/Wichita Heights in 1935. (Courtesy *The Wichita Eagle*.)

In her account of the day a tornado destroyed St. Mary's Academy, Sister M. Rosalia, C.S.J., wrote, "Mother's Day, May 10, 1942, was the day chosen by God to witness the passing of St. Mary of the Plains Academy, Dodge City. . . . As the girls filed out of the chapel, a hailstorm broke and the wind rose in fury; but windstorms were familiar visitors at St. Mary's, and nobody was worried about this. Ten minutes later, however, the blood-chilling shriek of the tornado filled the house, spreading terror and dismay. Its merciless force wrenched windows from their frames, dashed pictures from walls amid a hail of shattered glass. It tossed heavy pieces of furniture about as if they were mere toys. It lifted the roof from the venerable building, and crumbled walls as they fell inward. Within five minutes all was over; St. Mary's lay in ruins." (Quote used with permission of the Sisters of St. Joseph in Wichita, both courtesy Kansas Heritage Center.)

On April 9, 1947, a tornado outbreak began in Texas, devastated Woodward, Oklahoma, and continued into Kansas. Debris from near Woodward wound up in Barber County, Kansas. In Kansas, this same storm system ran west of Medicine Lodge before dissipating near St. Leo. (Courtesy Grant Hewitt, Donna Dreyer, and the McCormick family.)

Thurman Fussell, a survivor of the event who still lives in Woodward, described the effects of the tornado, "For weeks, even months following the storm people lived in tents, Army barracks west of town and with friends or relatives while they got their lives back together. My uncle and aunt kept an unclaimed baby for a few weeks until the parents were located. Doctors and medical staff from around the state drove in that night and the next day to give assistance. The Red Cross and other relief agencies assisted in many ways." (Courtesy Grant Hewitt, Donna Dreyer, and the McCormick family.)

On the evening of May 25, 1955, a massive storm erupted in Oklahoma, spawning a tornado that destroyed the eastern half of Blackwell, Oklahoma, at about 9:30 p.m. As the storm crossed the border into Kansas, it formed a second tornado that hit Udall around 10:30 p.m., leveling most of the town. Among the community's 500 residents, there were 77 fatalities and over 250 people were injured. This was the worst tornado to hit Udall, but it was not the first; the town also suffered damage from a twister that hit in 1909. (Above, courtesy Grant Hewitt; below, authors' collection.)

"Incredibly, as the sun rose the next morning on this tragedy, to the East remained the foundation of a house, the entire floor . . . a rug on the floor, dining room table with table cloth and in the center of the table . . . a fish bowl with fish swimming around inside. Nothing else remained of the dwelling," Dudley Toevs, at the time a student at Southwestern College, remembered the scene. (Above, Authors' collection; below, courtesy Grant Hewitt.)

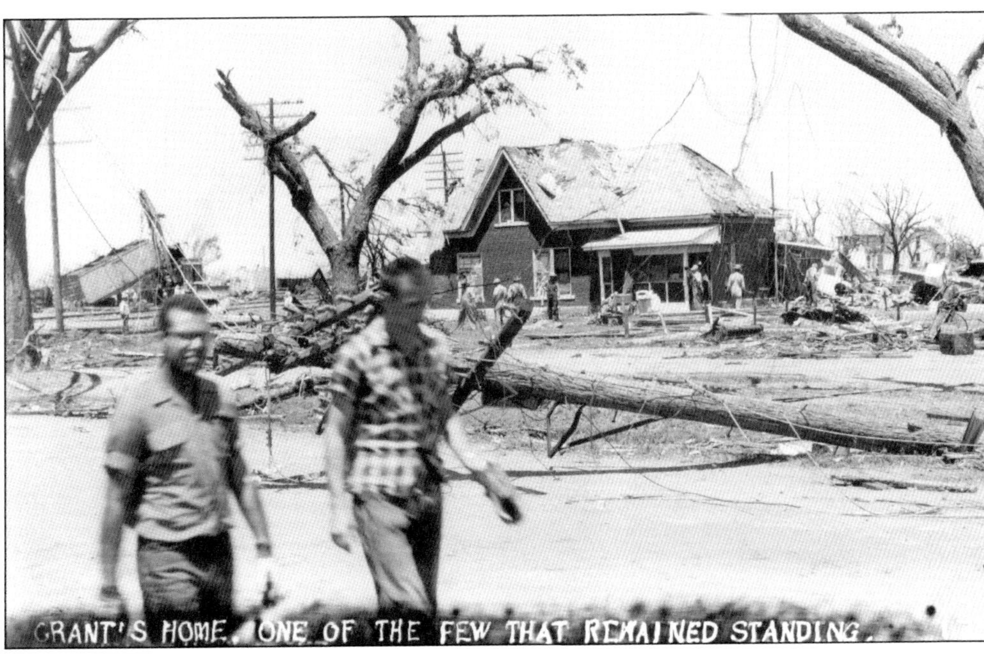

After the tornado, sightseers cluttered the roads to see what was left of Udall. Stan Finger and Phyllis Jacobs Griekspoor stated in the May 25, 1995 *Wichita Eagle*, "With the permission and assistance of Kansas Highway Patrol troopers, workers charged the gawkers $1 a car and raised $27,000 for Udall families, most of whom had no homeowners' insurance." (Both, courtesy Grant Hewitt.)

Although the gas station pictured here was not so lucky, one of the many oddities of the Udall tornado was that two Mobil Oil storage tanks survived the event intact. (Courtesy Grant Hewitt.)

Funerals served as emotional reminders of the tragedy. Here, services take place for 73-year-old Anna Carlson. The most touching funeral, however, was held for the five children of the King family, who were killed in their home in Oxford, Kansas, just before the tornado struck Udall. (Photograph by *Wichita Beacon*; courtesy *The Wichita Eagle*.)

"What didn't burn was shoved into a large hole and buried next to where the high school had been. Forty years later, tornado debris still works its way to the surface of what is now the Udall High School football field and practice lot," stated Stan Finger and Phyllis Jacobs Griekspoor in the May 25, 1995, *Wichita Eagle*. (Courtesy Udall Community Historical Museum.)

Members of the Wichita Association of Home Builders organized a crew of 50 to build a new city hall and community building for Udall. The structure was up by noon on May 27—a day and a half after the disaster. The following day, the building had telephones and electricity. (Courtesy *The Wichita Eagle*.)

Today, urban legend suggests erroneously that mobile homes actually attract tornadoes. In the 1950s, manufactured housing was seen as a promising solution for victims of disasters. This advertisement was part of a 1958 promotional newspaper endorsing the use of mobile homes. (Courtesy Udall Community Historical Museum.)

On June 10, 1958, a tornado ripped through the western end of El Dorado, Kansas, destroying four blocks of a new residential area along with Skelly Elementary School. The June 11, 1958, *Atchison Daily Globe* reported, "Some houses utterly disappeared leaving only foundations and the concrete floors of garages. Others lost only their roofs. In some cases a house seemed almost untouched although on either side there were total losses." (Courtesy *The Wichita Eagle*.)

As seen here, some residents were bewildered, while others searched the wreckage for survivors. Some people could only grieve, such as El Dorado resident John Daniels, who was working in Wichita when the tornado hit. Quoted in the June 11, 1958, *Wichita Eagle*, John said, "We went to my house first and there was nothing there—just a pile of timber. Then I ran to her [his wife] folks' house, 'cause I knew she went there a lot of times at night. Their house was flat too. We hurried to the police station and they sent me on to the Butler County 4-H Building where I identified them." Daniels lost his wife, one-year-old son, and his wife's parents. Seven other individuals died at Skelly Elementary School (below), where they had taken shelter from the storm. (Both, courtesy *The Wichita Eagle*.)

This image shows the aftermath of a tornado that hit the northeastern part of Wichita in 1965, resulting in 27 injuries and $2.5 million in property damages. (Courtesy *The Wichita Eagle*.)

Tornadoes do not discriminate on the basis of class; the 1965 Wichita tornado struck one of the city's more affluent neighborhoods. This photograph was taken during the process of residents recovering belongings from the rubble. (Courtesy *The Wichita Eagle*.)

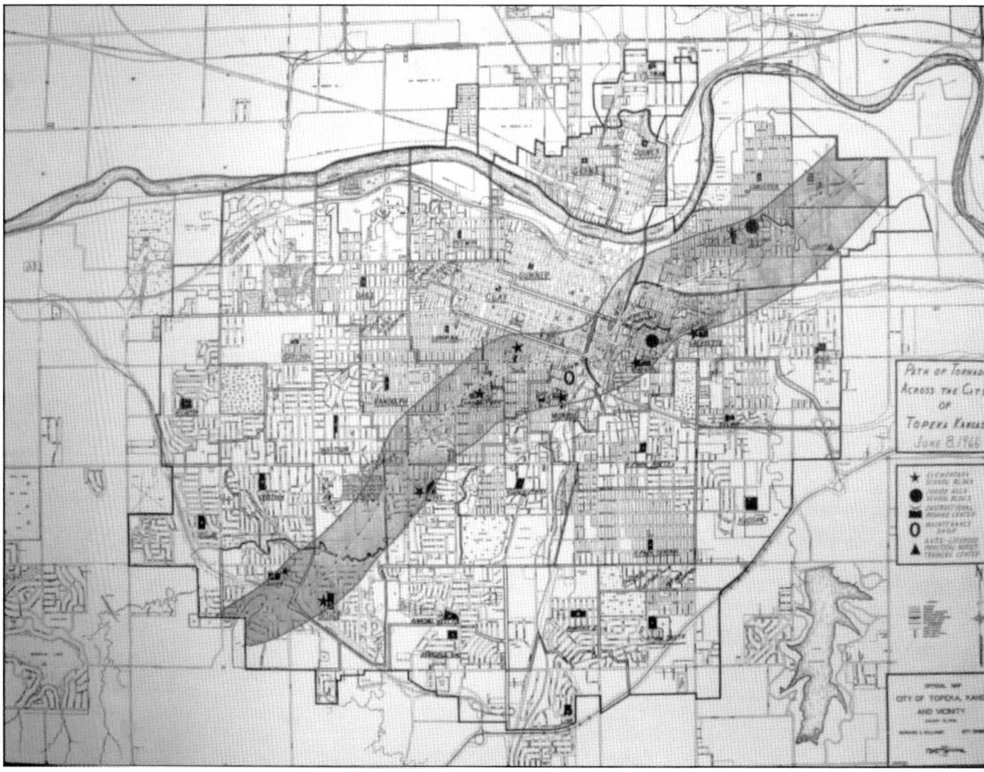

On June 8, 1966, north central Kansas experienced a series of tornadic storms. Manhattan received the first blow. At about 7:00 p.m., an F5 tornado formed near the southwestern corner of Shawnee County and proceeded to the northeast. (Courtesy Topeka Shawnee County Public Library.)

Television journalist Bill Kurtis has had a long and famous career, and the moment that started it off was when he was anchoring the WIBW news on June 8, 1966, and warned, "For God's Sake, Take Cover!" This image depicts the tornado bearing down on Topeka. (Courtesy *Topeka Capital-Journal*.)

Potawatomi chief Abram Burnett was buried at the base of a mound to the south of what became Topeka. Local legend said that as long as Burnett's Mound was undisturbed, Topeka would be safe from tornadoes. In 1960, the city constructed a water tank on the side of the mound; six years later, an F5 tornado came over the mound and hit Topeka. (Courtesy Keith Wondra.)

After the tornado passed over Burnett's Mound, it struck the housing developments and apartments on Twilight Drive, Twenty-ninth Street, and Gage Boulevard. Witnesses recalled houses being smashed and scattered across the landscape like trash. (Courtesy *Topeka Capital-Journal*.)

The path of the Topeka tornado led it directly onto the campus of Washburn University. One building that sustained severe damage was Rice Hall, the site of Topeka's first weather station. After the event, there was a proposal that the school should adopt a new, tornado-themed mascot—an idea that never came to pass. (Courtesy *The Wichita Eagle*.)

Still featuring the words "a refuge in time of storm," the National Reserve Life Insurance Building is pictured here with the ruins of the Pla-Land bowling alley in the foreground. In Bonar Menninger's book *And Hell Followed with It*, Gary Fleenor recalled that the 10-story landmark "shook violently as the tornado squeezed and seemed to tighten its grip like an anaconda crushing a large mammal." (Courtesy *Topeka Capital-Journal*.)

After the tornado hit Washburn University, it headed northeast toward downtown Topeka. The tornado's path is clearly visible here. After scratching the statehouse dome, the tornado made its way toward the Santa Fe Railroad Shops and Billard Airport. (Courtesy *Topeka Capital-Journal.*)

As Topekans started to rebuild, companies and organizations from across the state arrived to restore services. Here, Kansas Power and Light trucks arrive in a storm-damaged area. Because so many residents were literally on the doorsteps of churches needing help, the community's recently founded Doorstep social service organization became a much-appreciated institution. (Courtesy Westar Energy, Inc.)

On March 13, 1990, a tornado tore through the town of Hesston, Kansas. As the cyclone left Hesston behind, it began to weaken; meanwhile, a new tornado formed on a parallel track. The second tornado eventually absorbed the first one and continued northeast towards Goessel, Kansas. (Above, courtesy *The Wichita Eagle*; below, Duane Graham.)

In the shadow of the water tower that stood its ground during the storm, Hesston residents were determined to remain with their community. Resident Dave Patterson remarked, "All the help everyone received was quick and beneficial. People stayed during the rebuilding and saw it through." (Above, courtesy Duane Graham; below, American Red Cross Midway-Kansas Chapter.)

Late in the afternoon of April 26, 1991, as Wichitans were preparing to go home for the day, a severe storm developed over Harper County, Kansas, producing a tornado that tore across the city's southern flank from the southwest to the northeast. Its first target was Haysville before it slammed into McConnell Air Force Base (shown in these images). The tornado had grown into an F5 when it hit Andover in its final, deadliest phase, killing a total of 20 people. (Both, courtesy 22nd Air Refueling Wing.)

Although the installation's aircraft survived, many of the buildings on McConnell Air Force Base did not. Housing areas, recreation facilities, businesses, and even the base hospital took a direct hit. (Courtesy 22nd Air Refueling Wing.)

Andover resident Christopher Robrahn remembered, "There was a calm in the air with almost a slight fog. You heard no noises from nature, no birds, insects . . . nothing . . . only the sounds of sirens on their way to the damaged areas." (Courtesy 22nd Air Refueling Wing.)

A 10-minute warning spared McConnell loss of life. This American flag was a sign that the installation would rebuild. Today, the tornado is part of the installation's lore; the officers and enlisted club is called the "Storm Cellar." (Courtesy 22nd Air Refueling Wing.)

Wichita resident Cheryl Huggins, although not in the tornado's path, remembered, "After the tornado, the parents of one of my orthopedic patients received a set of report cards in the mail. A couple in Topeka found the person's Wichita High School report cards in their backyard, located the parents, and sent the cards back." (Courtesy Sedgwick County, Kansas, Emergency Management.)

The Andover tornado devastated over 1,500 residences, including 400 units at the Golden Spur Mobile Home Park. A number of homes in Andover did not have basements, forcing residents to take shelter in inner rooms. One couple survived the event by taking shelter in this closet. (Courtesy Sedgwick County, Kansas, Emergency Management.)

Natural disasters like tornadoes can lure public figures and the media as well as emergency response teams, as shown in these two photographs from the Andover aftermath. Above, Elizabeth Dole (second from right), who was the president of the American Red Cross at the time, talks to a reporter. Below, Kansas Gov. Joan Finney (center) views the damage. Visits such as these can draw attention to the needs of communities, but they can also disrupt relief efforts and interfere with residents who may still be struggling to make sense of what happened. (Above, courtesy American Red Cross Midway-Kansas Chapter; below, Sedgwick County, Kansas, Emergency Management.)

On May 3, 1999, a series of storms developed in northern Oklahoma and southern Kansas. In Sumner County, a storm dropped a tornado that grew into an F5 and swept across Haysville, killing five and injuring 100. (Courtesy Sedgwick County, Kansas, Emergency Management.)

The May 1999 tornado destroyed Haysville's historic downtown district but saved its greatest devastation for south Wichita in the area between MacArthur and Seneca streets. (Courtesy Sedgwick County, Kansas, Emergency Management.)

These photographs offer before-and-after views of a home in the path of the May 1999 Haysville tornado. The family living in the home survived, along with four of their six dogs. One day after the tornado, the furnace ignited a fire that destroyed what was left. (Both, courtesy Susan McCoy.)

The region between south Wichita and Haysville contained many mobile home parks, including the Lakeshore and Pacesetter Mobile Home Parks and the Silver Spur, pictured here. (Courtesy American Red Cross Midway-Kansas Chapter.)

In *Flyover People*, author Cheryl Unruh writes, "Our happy-go-lucky sky betrayed us, but the wounds inflicted became badges of survival and strength." (Courtesy American Red Cross Midway-Kansas Chapter.)

On April 21, 2001, a series of thunderstorms developed over Pawnee County and moved to the northeast throughout the evening. Although there were severe thunderstorm warnings by 10:00 p.m., it was too dark to see the tornado that eventually hit Hoisington. Tornado sirens went off after the event happened. The storm devastated homes and businesses and frightened students who were attending the high school's prom. (Both, courtesy *The Wichita Eagle*.)

The night of May 4, 2007, an EF5 "wedge" tornado roared across Kiowa County, leveling almost all of Greensburg. Although similar in size to the Udall tornado, the one that hit Greensburg caused 9 deaths, compared to 77 in Udall. Those who study weather, such as Mike Smith of WeatherData, have concluded that improved warning systems literally made the difference between life and death. (Courtesy *The Wichita Eagle*.)

Greensburg residents were shocked and stunned by what happened but were determined to move forward, as these statements mixing pride and humor attest. The disaster gained nationwide attention, including the support of actor Leonardo DiCaprio. Rebuilding continues to be a challenge, however; only half of the town's pre-2007 population remains today. (Above, courtesy Emilie Petersen; below, *The Wichita Eagle*.)

Prior to the tornado, Greensburg's claim to fame was a museum that featured the largest hand-dug well and a 1,000-pound pallasite meteorite. The cover to the well survived, but the rest of the museum did not. The meteorite was found in the rubble and was put on display at Wichita's Exploration Place, where donations helped Greensburg survivors. (Courtesy Emilie Petersen.)

"The couple's daughter had killed the deer with a bow and arrow when she was about eight years old and had received some attention for being the youngest hunter to do so . . . this specific item was the one thing that they were attached to at the time and I'm really glad it was something they could keep," emergency responder Emilie Petersen, describing her work in the community a few days following the disaster. (Courtesy Emilie Petersen.)

Townspeople have come together for the first town meeting following the Greensburg tornado. About 700 people were in attendance at the event, which took place only days after the storm. This photograph was taken by Rex Harris, a member of the KAKE-Channel 10 news team. (Courtesy Rex Harris.)

In the wake of the tornado, Greensburg began to transform itself into a "green" community, paying special attention to resource conservation. Architecture students from the University of Kansas helped to design and construct the 5.4.7 Arts Center, the first public structure completed during the rebuilding effort. (Courtesy Jay M. Price.)

Tornadoes continue to shape lives in Kansas. On May 21, 2011, severe weather about 50 miles south of Topeka produced the above tornado as well as an EF3 tornado that destroyed most of Reading, Kansas, a town with a population of about 250, seen below shortly after the event. It was the first major tornadic event in the state that year—one that was eclipsed by the massive devastation of Joplin in neighboring Missouri. (Above, courtesy Mallory Medvene; below, Andrea Holt.)

In recent years, the Great Plains' reputation for tornadoes has become an attraction as much as a source of fear. Companies such as Tempest Tours now conduct guided sojourns for people to observe severe weather and tornadoes from a relatively safe distance. Here, a tour group in Kansas waits to catch a glimpse of a twister. (Courtesy Tempest Tours.)

Reflecting both the beneficial and destructive power of moving air, a tornado skirts a group of wind turbines in Kansas in 2008. (Photograph by Sean Waugh; courtesy NOAA Photograph Library, NOAA's NSSL Collection.)

With the onset of civil defense systems after World War II, the now-familiar sirens that warn citizens of severe weather became parts of the Kansas landscape. This siren is likely Federal Signal Corporation's "Thunderbolt" model, a design that first came out in 1952. (Courtesy Sedgwick County, Kansas, Emergency Management.)

Three

Living with the Monster

Before modern meteorology, the average person relied mainly on folklore and tradition when it came to preparing for tornadoes. A passage on storms and climate in the 1912 *Kansas Cyclopedia* noted that several dry years in the 1880s had numerous twisters while the wet years had few, concluding that tornadoes were a function of a dry climate. Still advocating the "rain follows the plow" thesis, the author assumed confidently that cultivation of the land was bringing more moisture to the local climate and thus tornadoes "in a few years . . . will be a thing of the past." Such optimism proved to be tragically wrong.

The first official monitoring of weather, including tornadoes, occurred in the 1800s under the guidance of the Smithsonian Institution. In 1873, the Army's Signal Corps took on that responsibility. In 1877, Lt. John P. Finley joined the Signal Corps' training program and became one of the first individuals to systematically study tornadoes, researching the 1879 Marshall County, Kansas, tornado outbreak. In 1891, weather monitoring and forecasting shifted to the US Weather Bureau, an agency that functioned initially under the Department of Agriculture and later, after 1940, the Department of Commerce. In a 1970 restructuring, the Weather Bureau became the National Weather Service, governed under the National Oceanographic and Atmospheric Administration.

There is a complicated history behind informing the public about potential tornadoes. Until the 1960s, the Weather Bureau had a strict policy not to use the term "tornado" in its public warnings, fearing the word would cause panic. Today, a network of organizations, agencies, media outlets, and companies monitor severe weather, inform the population about tornadic threats, and help people and communities rebuild after a twister strikes. Despite these advances, meteorologists still struggle to give residents in Tornado Alley proper advance warnings of tornadoes. The greatest challenge is encouraging average citizens to adequately prepare themselves for severe weather and to respond in ways that help rather than hinder relief and rescue efforts.

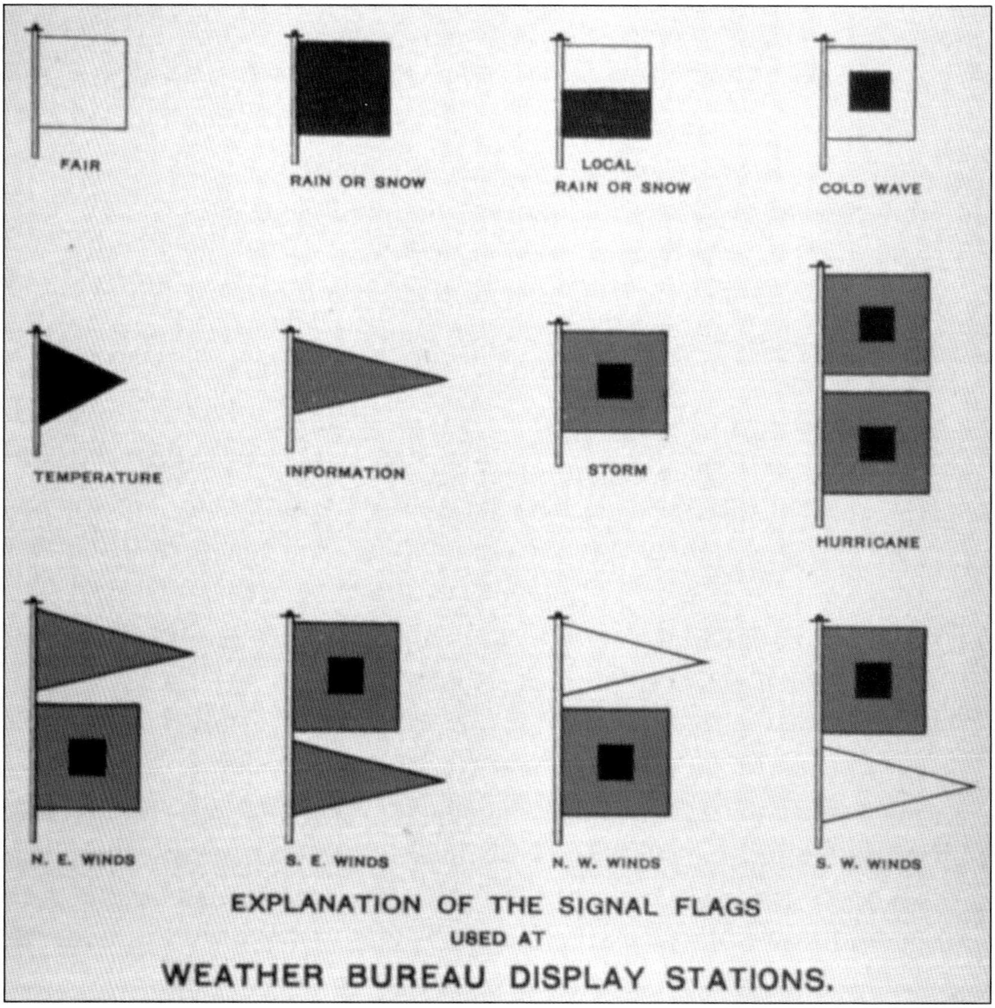

Initially, weather bureau stations conveyed forecasts by raising a series of flags, largely indicating if warmer or cooler weather was to come. The arrival of radio reduced the need for flags on land-based weather stations. Elements of this system remain on the coasts, however, such as a pair of red flags with black squares connoting hurricanes. (Archival photograph by Sean Linehan, NOS, NGS; courtesy NOAA.)

On June 1, 1887, the Signal Corps established a station in Rice Hall at Washburn University in Topeka. Sgt. T.B. Jennings was the first "meteorologist in charge" of this operation. (Courtesy National Weather Service Topeka, Kansas Weather Forecast Office.)

Meteorologist Snowden Dwight Flora came to Kansas in 1905 to work for the Topeka Weather Bureau. In 1917, he became the director of the office and served until 1949. His 1953 book *Tornadoes of the United States* was the first major work on the subject and remained a key text for several generations of meteorologists and storm spotters. (Courtesy National Weather Service Topeka, Kansas Weather Forecast Office.)

Established in 1905, the weather station in Iola was the first in Kansas to have its own specially constructed building. Built in 1908, this structure housed the family of the observer as well as equipment. The observer provided weather data to Chicago via telegraph and, in return, conveyed weather forecasts to the community. The office remained open until 1936. (Courtesy NOAA.)

The US Signal Corps established an office in Dodge City in 1875, when observations took place and signals were sent from the roof of the Dodge House. Later, the office moved to the Beeson Building, which is shown here. (Courtesy National Weather Service Dodge City, Kansas Weather Forecast Office.)

The Goodland weather station, initially located at the First National Bank, began in 1895. It changed locations several times before 1919, when attorney Frank Horton (seen here) became the observer and started operating the weather station out of his home. Horton served as observer until 1943. (Courtesy National Weather Service Goodland, Kansas Weather Forecast Office.)

In late 1943, the Goodland weather station moved to Renner Field. The relationship between weather and aviation continued to develop after the war, with all weather stations in the state eventually located at or near airports. (Courtesy National Weather Service Goodland, Kansas Weather Forecast Office.)

The first weather bureau office in Concordia opened in 1885 and was closely connected with the local postmaster. In 1914, the office moved to the new courthouse, shown here with the equipment on the roof. (Courtesy Marvin and Eudora Petersen.)

The Concordia office was a modest affair, issuing weather forecasts by raising flags and even by sending postcards. Like many small weather stations, Concordia began as a one-person operation that was not staffed on evenings and weekends. After a tornado struck while the office was closed, Gov. Frank Carlson decided to make Concordia a 24-hour operation. (Courtesy Marvin and Eudora Petersen.)

In 1962, a new facility (seen here) opened at the Concordia airport. By the 1990s, Doppler radar technology had eliminated the need for many small weather stations. In a wave of consolidation, smaller stations such as Concordia closed while larger stations like Wichita took on the responsibility for weather in central Kansas. (Courtesy Jay M. Price.)

Marvin Petersen and his wife, Eudora, moved to Concordia to help staff the station full-time. Like a number of weather bureau figures at the time, Petersen received his meteorology training through the Air Force's Air Weather Service. (Courtesy Jay M. Price.)

In this 1958 photograph, Gordon Wylie (left), who arrived from Hawai'i to take over as meteorologist in charge of Wichita's weather office, shakes hands with outgoing meteorologist-in-charge Vic Phillips. Under Wylie, the office embarked on early storm-spotter training, as well as a test of Doppler radar technology. (Courtesy National Weather Service Wichita, Kansas, Weather Forecast Office, and *The Wichita Eagle*.)

Weatherman Cecil Carrier (standing) chats with Clarence Hill at the National Weather Service office in Wichita. Remembering Carrier's influence, *The Wichita Eagle*'s Stan Finger recalled, "For many residents of the Wichita area, he was weather's Walter Cronkite: a voice you could trust in the midst of the confusion." (Courtesy National Weather Service Wichita, Kansas, Weather Forecast Office, and *The Wichita Eagle*.)

This 1962 radar image from the Topeka weather station shows a telltale "hook echo," which suggests strong rotation in a storm. (Courtesy NOAA.)

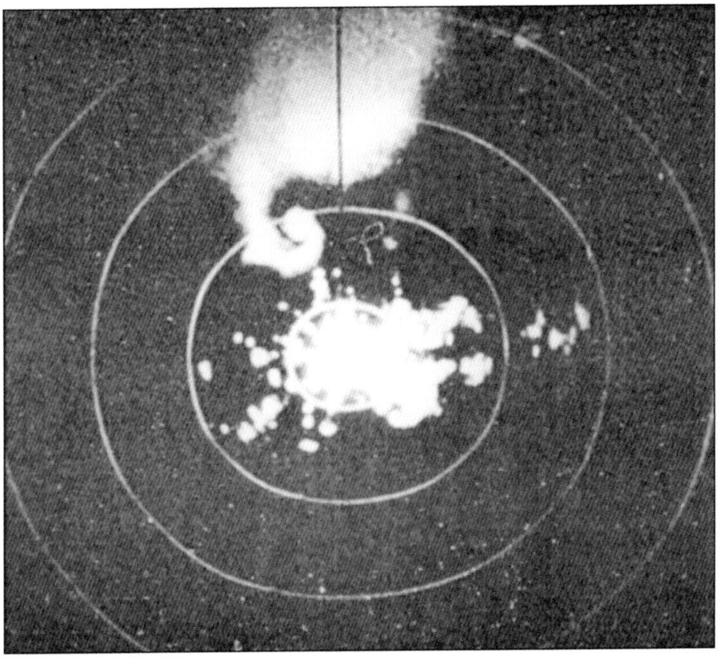

This is a Doppler on Wheels radar image of a 2008 tornado in Quinter, Kansas. The tornado is at the tip of a hook echo at the edge of a supercell thunderstorm. The circle in the center of the hook shows the debris lifted by the tornado. (Courtesy Joshua Wurman, Center for Severe Weather Research.)

The arrival of Doppler radar brought dramatically better images of storms and their structures. Above, a crew installs a WSR-57 radar at Wichita Mid-Continent Airport; it was the predecessor of the WSR-88D radar now in use. Below, the radar located in Haven, Kansas, belongs to television station KSN and was the most powerful Doppler radar in the state when it was erected. (Above, courtesy National Weather Service Wichita, Kansas; below, Sadonia Corns.)

Wichita's National Weather Service Station was one of the first in the nation to use Doppler radar. This experimental project began in 1959 but was of limited use in detecting severe weather. Full-scale Doppler use did not take place until the 1990s. (Courtesy National Weather Service Wichita, Kansas Weather Forecast Office.)

When Wichita's Exploration Place opened in 1999, the facility included a "weather lab," where staff from KSN worked while the public could watch through large windows. Seen here from left to right are KSN meteorologists Mark Bogner, Rodney Price, Dave Schaffer, and Dave Freeman talking to a group of visitors. KSN issued weather broadcasts from the facility for nearly a decade. (Courtesy Exploration Place.)

Tinker Air Force Base in Oklahoma City helped launch modern tornado warnings when it received hits from two tornadoes in 1948. Col. Robert C. Miller, USAF (Ret.) remembered, "At 10 p.m. (March 20, 1948), the large tornado, visible in a vivid background of continuous lightning began moving from the southwest to northeast across the base . . . it passed just east of the large hangars and the operations building where we crouched in near panic. Suddenly the glass in the control tower to our right succumbed." (Courtesy NOAA and Tinker Air Force Base.)

On March 25, 1948, US Air Force meteorologists Robert C. Miller and Ernest Fawbush noticed weather patterns similar to those of March 20. Following their analysis, the commander at Tinker issued the first operational tornado warning just before a second twister struck the base, causing the damage seen in the photographs on this page. Regular tornado warnings for the general public did not occur until much later. (Courtesy NOAA and Tinker Air Force Base.)

"No, it wasn't an H-bomb that struck Udall. . . . It was a tornado," reads a clipping found at the Udall Community Historical Society. After the 1955 Udall tornado, the community built a watchtower that had two people staffing it from dawn to dusk every day. It lasted for about 20 years and is now the press box for the high school football field. (Courtesy Udall Community Historical Museum.)

WELLINGTON, KANSAS, MONDAY,

DISCUSSING NETWORK of storm spotters in Sumner County are these local officials and Wichita weathermen. Seated are (left to right) Theron Sallee, meteorologist, Mayor J. M. Slaten and W. Gordon Wylie, meteorologist in charge of the Wichita Weather Bureau. Standing are Jim Chase, chairman of the Oklahoma-Kansas Storm Spotters Service Council; Vernon Clark, Wellington-Sumner County Civil Defense director and Ellis Pike, meteorologist. — (Daily News Photo)

In March 1959, the first official storm-spotter training class in the area was held in Wellington, Kansas. A total of 225 people attended, coming from as far east as Fort Scott and as far west as Pretty Prairie, as well as from a few Oklahoma cities. (Courtesy *Wellington Daily News*.)

As civil defense became part of everyday life, "duck-and-cover drills," along with sirens, shelters, and networks of officials, were developed to assist the public in case of attack from the Soviet Union. These precautions also lent themselves to assisting the public in the event of severe weather. (Both, courtesy Sedgwick County, Kansas, Emergency Management.)

Filmmaker Sean Casey created the "Tornado Intercept Vehicle" (TIV) to withstand the direct hit of a small- to medium-sized twister. Casey headed a team with meteorologist Brandon Ivey (left) and driver/mechanic/medic Marcus Gutierrez (right), shown here with the TIV at an event at Hutchinson's Cosmophere. Ivey, a Kansan, became interested in meteorology after learning about the Hesston tornado as a child. (Photograph by Greg Holmes, courtesy Kansas Cosmosphere.)

The availability of weather maps and radar images online, coupled with wireless Internet access, allows storm chasers such as Bryce Kintigh (passenger seat) and Justin Dean (driver's seat) to track storms in the field. In addition to offering chase tours, Kintigh provides live updates to KAKE-TV during severe weather. (Courtesy Jay M. Price.)

In the 1970s, the National Weather Service in Kansas decided to focus on severe weather and dropped its climatology office. Dean Bark, professor of physics at Kansas State University, worked to save the climate data library and had it transferred to the university. Among Bark's research was a study of the 1966 tornadic events that struck Manhattan early in the day before later devastating Topeka. Mary Knapp, pictured at Kansas State University, has served as state climatologist since 1992. (Courtesy Mary Knapp.)

Remembering the Ruskin Heights tornado of his youth, Mike Smith went on to pursue a career in weather prediction, developing the green-yellow-orange-red color palette used in weather radar images. His company, WeatherData, is located in Wichita and specializes in weather prediction services for business and institutional clients. (Courtesy Jay M. Price.)

Conventional wisdom once recommended opening windows in the face of an oncoming storm to moderate the sudden change in pressure when a tornado hit and, presumably, reduce structural damage. This surviving frame indicates that this window from a house in Wichita was not open when the twister struck in 1965. Current research suggests the practice does very little to save buildings. (Courtesy *The Wichita Eagle*.)

The Skywarn program, in which teams of local storm spotters monitor conditions near their respective communities and report information to National Weather Service (NWS) officials, began in the 1960s. In return, the NWS distributes weather information through local bodies such as police, fire, or emergency management departments. (Authors' collection.)

Wichita radio station KFDI initially sent out reporters to cover traffic reports, but manager Jim Setters found that the system also worked well for severe weather coverage. By the 1970s, the station was sending out trained spotters who used two-way radios to stay in contact with the station. Occasionally, the station gets the comment, "I hate country music, but I listen to KFDI for the weather." (Courtesy KFDI.)

When severe weather strikes, the studio at KFDI becomes a hub of activity. John Wright, shown here, was in a mobile unit just outside of Hesston when the 1990 tornado hit—his coverage of the event earned the station an Edward R. Murrow Award. (Courtesy KFDI.)

News stations in Wichita, which serve all of central and western Kansas, have earned reputations for particularly thorough weather coverage, even when compared to other cities in Tornado Alley. Since 2002, KFDI has had a relationship with KWCH's weather team. Pictured here are, from left to right, Phil White, George Lawson, Mark Larson, Wil Day, John Wright, Dan Dillon, John O'Hara, Merril Teller, Marc LaVoie, Ross Janssen, and Rodney Price. (Courtesy KFDI and KWCH.)

In 1966, WIBW was Topeka's only television station. Today, there are several that provide weather coverage to northeastern Kansas. WIBW meteorologist Drew Switzer, a Missouri native, shares the opinion of many who study and report severe weather, wishing that "people in both states would take warnings, especially tornado warnings, more seriously." (Courtesy WIBW.)

While meteorologists study the dynamics of tornadoes, federal, state, and local governmental bodies help educate the general population about how to react to tornado warnings. In 1982, Wayne Speigel prepared this booklet for the Kansas Division of Emergency Preparedness. Tom Fisher's illustrations used the characters of *The Wizard of Oz* to teach tornado safety. This booklet is part of a collection at the Topeka Shawnee County Public Library. (Courtesy Kansas Adjutant General's Department.)

In the aftermath of a tornado, the National Guard is often called to assist in a variety of functions. Working with local officials, it can assist in search and rescue, security, logistics, and aviation support. In this photograph, the National Guard has been called to help with the 1990 Hesston tornado. (Courtesy Duane Graham.)

Immediately after a disaster strikes, first-response teams arrive. In this case, individuals from the American Red Cross go into an area to survey the needs of victims and their families. Shortly after, a second set of teams arrives to provide information about services and programs that can help. Here, a team helps victims of the 1999 Haysville tornado. (Courtesy American Red Cross Midway-Kansas chapter.)

Addie E. Pearson prepares food in the wake of the Hesston tornado. (Courtesy American Red Cross Midway-Kansas chapter.)

The Salvation Army also plays a major role in assisting victims of tornadoes in Kansas, as well as responders and volunteers who are there to help. Here, the Salvation Army provides food in the wake of the Haysville tornado. (Courtesy Susan McCoy.)

Jillian Overstake (right) helps victims of a 2003 tornado in Franklin, Kansas. (Courtesy Grant Overstake.)

Mennonites have long helped their neighbors in times of tragedy, and in 1950 a picnic of Mennonites in Hesston, Kansas, inspired the creation of an organized service to assist people in the wake of disasters. The group's early relief efforts included assisting victims of a tornado in Oklahoma as well as flood victims in Canada. The result was an entity called the Mennonite Service Organization, soon renamed the Mennonite Disaster Service. Above, Mennonite volunteers help search for personal items in Haysville. In the 1990 image below, a Mennonite Disaster Service bus in Hesston is ready to help the community where the organization first developed. (Above, courtesy Susan McCoy; below, Duane Graham.)

The Greensburg tornado was the first major project of the Kansas State Animal Response Team, which now has 20 chapters in the state. A team of responders, including Dr. Christen L. Skaer, took care of displaced or injured animals ranging from this horse and foal (seen with assistant Heather Phinney) to what Dr. Skaer described as "a cat that came in about 7 days after the tornado. The owners found it stuck in a drawer of a cabinet under rubble." (Courtesy Christen L. Skaer, D.V.M.)

Life in Tornado Alley includes stories of rebuilding as well as destruction. Here, a team of volunteers constructs a house in Greensburg. The recovery phase, which begins with the rebuilding process, can last for weeks, if not months. (Courtesy Jay M. Price.)

Storm shelters like this one in Haven, Kansas, serve as the setting for many stories across tornado alley. Recalling his childhood in Woodward, Oklahoma, Thurman Fussell reflected, "We spent many an evening, even many nights, in that cellar with all that canned food, which included fruit, vegetables and canned beef . . . while my father kept watch on the clouds." (Courtesy Sadonia Corns.)

Working with Federal Emergency Management Administration (FEMA) guidelines, as well the National Storm Shelter Association, companies like Protection Shelters create shelters for both households and communities. This community shelter is for Chapman, Kansas, which was hit by a tornado in 2008. (Courtesy Protection Shelters LLC.)

The back of this postcard reads, "Springfield Tornado Insurance offers the best protection against Tornado Damage. It is the PIONEER Tornado Company. For nearly forty years it has paid Tornado Damage claims—paid them in full, without discount. It is the Company of Prompt Service and the Square Deal. You cannot afford to be without Tornado Insurance." (Authors' collection.)

Life in Tornado Alley includes the ongoing challenge of constructing buildings that can withstand severe weather. The circular shape of R. Buckminster Fuller's Dymaxion House was supposed to be able to hold up to swirling winds. Only two prototypes were built, including this one in Wichita; neither of them faced the test of an actual tornado. (Courtesy Wichita-Sedgwick County Historical Museum.)

In 1956, David Hoadley started looking at storms and tornadoes as they were forming, and he has continued to do so each year since (except during his wedding and honeymoon). Raleigh Lackey, a meteorological technician working in south central Kansas, commented that Hoadley chased tornadoes the way other young men chased girls, a remark that may well be the origin of the term "storm chasing." Passionate about responsible study of severe weather out in the field, in 1977 Hoadley helped found a newsletter for severe weather spotters that eventually became the "Stormtrack" Internet forum. (Both, courtesy David Hoadley.)

Tornado Alley's reputation has come, in part, from art and popular culture that associates twisters with the region. Herschel C. Logan of Salina, Kansas, for example, depicted a tornado in a farm setting in this 1938 woodcut. (Courtesy Kansas State Historical Society.)

Four

AN ONGOING, TURBULENT RELATIONSHIP

Kansans are tuned in to the tornado. In addition to being destructive forces of nature, twisters can also be icons for residents of the Sunflower State. Sometimes tornadoes are meant to represent strength, as with school mascots. Twisters are also used to represent flowing movement and beauty, as shown within artistic works. The tornado has become a symbol for Kansas itself.

The ultimate reference to tornadoes in Kansas comes from L. Frank Baum's *The Wonderful Wizard of Oz*. Kansans are routinely asked if they have seen Dorothy or Toto or told, "You're not in Kansas any more!" The reply is usually a polite chuckle and a change in subject, sometimes even to a weather-related topic. The book and film may have used the tornado as a device to transport Dorothy away from Kansas to Oz, but in popular culture Oz, Kansas, and tornadoes are forever linked.

Even if they have never seen a tornado, Kansans find themselves remembering the impact of twisters on their state. Monuments to tornado victims can be simplistic, artistic, or both, while collections of personal items and photographs are memorials in their own rights.

Kansans and all who live in Tornado Alley incorporate severe weather and its effects into their daily lives, with its traces visible on the landscape even when the sky is clear. While other states receive a share of tornadoes, Kansas seems to embrace—or has been forced to embrace—the twister as one of its most powerful symbols.

In large part, Kansas owes its reputation for tornadoes to someone who never lived in the state. L. Frank Baum's *The Wonderful Wizard of Oz*, published in 1900, uses the tornado to transport Dorothy Gale from Kansas to the mythical land of Oz. MGM's 1939 movie based on Baum's work has helped *The Wizard of Oz* become the state's most identifiable theme. (Courtesy Library of Congress.)

Today, the Oz/tornado/Kansas theme helps market a host of institutions. Even the Kansas Underground Salt Museum in Hutchinson uses the imagery—in this case, on a T-shirt that visitors can purchase in the museum's gift shop. (Courtesy Kansas Underground Salt Museum.)

When John Steuart Curry received the commission for the murals in the Topeka State House, he did not shrink from depicting the twister. In *The Tragic Prelude*, which depicts the volatile 1850s and 1860s, an era called "Bleeding Kansas," Curry created a fiery John Brown with a tornado in the background. Curry's murals were controversial, as many Kansans did not want their state associated with such destructive imagery. (Courtesy Jay M. Price.)

After the tornado, Udall began the process of rebuilding even before the rubble had been cleared. Within three years, there were 191 new homes, and the downtown area had 21 businesses. As this license plate states, "Udall, Kansas is still on the map." (Photograph by Keith Wondra, courtesy Udall Community Historical Museum.)

The Codell tornadoes are memorialized in this wall hanging that depicts the history of Rooks County, Kansas. (Photograph by Keith Wondra; courtesy Rooks County Historical Museum.)

In spite of its devastating reputation, locals sometimes embrace the funnel cloud as a mascot. When Scott MacDonald decided to open a bar and grill in Colby, Kansas, he figured it would be hit by a tornado at some time and dubbed it "Twisters." Twisters II is in WaKeeney, Kansas. To date, the name actually seems to have warded off the tornado threat, and both places are popular hangouts for local storm chasers. (Courtesy Jay M. Price.)

The image of the twister can even be found in the world of beverages. Dan Norton, head brewer of River City Brewing Company, explained, "Back in 2004, we decided to put an India Pale Ale on our permanent beer menu . . . so, since we are located in the heart of Tornado Alley, and tornadoes are aggressive and this beer is aggressive, it seemed like a natural fit. We had our staff vote on five different names, and Tornado Alley IPA won." (Courtesy River City Brewing Company, Wichita, Kansas.)

Although never in a tornado himself, Wichita Wes Race had found twisters a part of his life from a young age. A tornado destroyed his father's family home in Omaha. He also saw the damage in northeast Wichita the night of the 1965 tornado. In 1983, Wes got into a conversation with musician Jerry Woods about why trailer parks seemed to be "tornado bait"; the result was the poem below. Just recently, Wes got a tornado tattoo.

All the mobile homes are huddled
On the outskirts of town
With their radios turned on
Wishin' they were underground
'Cause a surrealistic dandy
About one mile high
Had made up his mind
To jump out of the southwestern sky
Tornado bait!
We've been livin' on the moment
With our wide open play;
Actin' real naughty
Has been the order of the day
Our false pleasures getting
More expensive every day;
The sudden shock of recognition
Has blown us all away
Tornado bait!
Tornado bait party,
It's a Midwestern affair
Tornado bait party,
It's been an all day bash
Tornado bait party,
I just heard some windows crash
Tornado bait party,
Everybody's in the groove
Tornado bait party,
I just felt the trailer move
Tornado bait party,
Smack dab in the whirlwind's path
Tornado bait party,
Not thinkin' about the aftermath

After Race wrote his poem, he, Woods, and Jim Young, the owner of a local Blues club called The Spot, set up the first "Tornado Bait Party" at the club. After The Spot closed, Dave Strough, owner of the Shamrock Lounge, stepped forward to continue the annual tradition held every May that is part music festival, part costume contest, and part dark humor party—complete with EMS-themed decorations. At right, the third Tornado Bait Party is advertised on an actual NOAA tornado warning poster. (At right, courtesy Wes Race; below, Keith Wondra.)

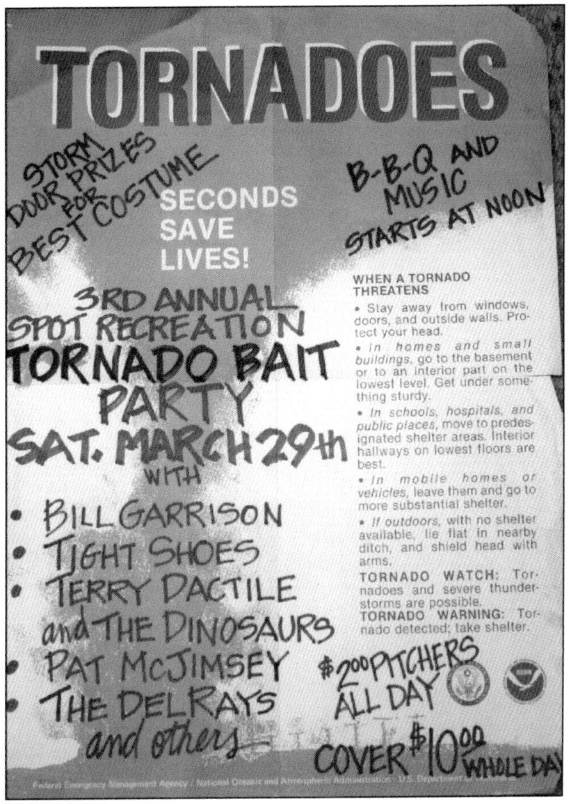

During the 2010 fall football season, the Eureka High School Tornadoes booster club paired up with KAKE meteorologist Jay Prater and came up with the motivation needed to amp up their players and fans; at the beginning of each game, a tornado warning is issued. Of course, it's not a real warning—except for the opposing team. (Courtesy Nancy Corns.)

Recalling on the strength of a tornado seen near the school as it was being constructed, the Golden Tornado (or "Golden 'Nado") became the mascot for Field Kindley High School in Coffeyville, Kansas, in 1931. (Courtesy Russell Shields and James Dodge.)

In the 1940s, the O.A. Sutton Company came out with an electric fan series called the "Vornado." Model 38, shown here, was a popular version from the 1950s. In 1959, the Two Guys discount store chain acquired A.O. Sutton and named the new company Vornado. The company continued fan business until the early 1980s. In 1989, a new Vornado Fan Company in Andover, Kansas, carried on the tradition. (Courtesy Vornado Fan Company.)

The "Tornado" amusement park ride, shown here at the Kansas State Fair in September 2010, is owned and operated by North American Midway Entertainment. Riders are circulated simultaneously around the axis of the pod in which they sit and also the base of the contraption. (Courtesy Jessica C. Nellis.)

Printing students at Wichita State University formed a guild called the Tornado Alley Press (TAP) to create artwork as a group. The group decided on the name "Tornado Alley Press" as a way to hearken back to one of the nationally recognized icons of Kansas. (Courtesy Tornado Alley Press.)

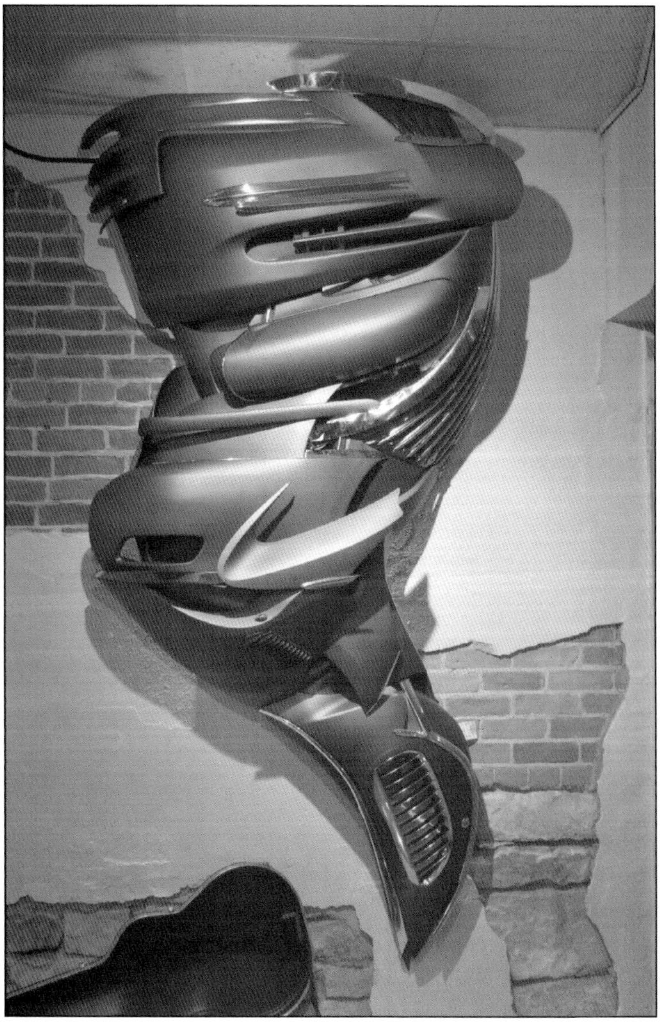

Wichita-based artist Greg Johnson created this sculpture, called *Twister*, using car parts. Johnson draws on years of experience with automotive collisions to create his works of art and currently has two other tornado-themed sculptures underway. Johnson's website (gregjohnsonsculpture.com) describes the tornado as "both a menacing, unpredictable, destructive and deadly example of nature's wrath, as well as a dynamic, beautiful, exciting and powerful natural phenomenon." (Photograph by Jessica C. Nellis, courtesy Greg Johnson.)

When Chinese artist Hong Zhang moved to Lawrence, she found herself fascinated with the region's tornadic legacy. In this piece, called *Twister*, Zhang fuses the depiction of a woman's long hair, a motif found in Chinese art, with the structure of the tornado. This piece is on display at the Ulrich Museum on the Wichita State University campus. (Courtesy Hong Zhang and Ulrich Museum of Art, Wichita State University.)

In 1978, artist Rockne Krebs created a sculpture entitled *Tornado* to grace the atrium of the Frank Carlson Federal Building in Topeka. Early plans gave the piece various names, including *White Light*, *White Rainbow*, *White Twister*, and *The White Tornado*. (Courtesy Jay M. Price.)

To mark the 20th anniversary of the Andover tornado, the city council set up tables in the chambers and covered them with unclaimed photographs over several days in late April 2011. That evening, as they picked through the musty stacks, a number of individuals were reunited with family mementos that had been lost for decades. (Courtesy Jay M. Price.)

Cyclone Lane in southern Marshall County crosses the path of the 1879 Irving tornado, although there is no evidence that this was intentional; when the 9-1-1 emergency system began, the county needed to have a C-named road at that location. (Courtesy Jay M. Price.)

Following the devastating Udall tornado of 1955, residents erected this memorial in the city park. (Courtesy Keith Wondra.)

The memorial in the Topeka Cemetery is dedicated to the citizens who helped the city return to normalcy after June 8, 1966. The memorial is also dedicated to the 16 people who died. (Courtesy Keith Wondra.)

Ross Barrable designed the 1958 Tornado Victims Memorial, located at Graham Park in El Dorado. The memorial consists of 13 pillars, each representing a casualty of the tornado, surrounding a swooping statue topped with an Aeolian harp. (Courtesy Philip H. Nellis.)

Greensburg, Kansas, continues to rebuild after its devastating May 2007 tornado. At the Big Well, where the attraction's visitors' center was among the structures leveled, this sculpture commemorates the town's destruction—and its indestructible spirit. (Courtesy Jay M. Price.)

Bibliography

Beemer, Rod. *The Deadliest Woman in the West: Mother Nature on the Prairies and Plains 1800–1900*. Caldwell, ID: Caxton Press, 2006.

Biles, Jan and Will Kennedy, eds. *Topeka Remembers: A Personalized History of the Capital City*. Topeka: *Topeka Capital-Journal*, 2003.

Bluestein, Howard B. *Tornado Alley: Monster Storms of the Great Plains*. New York: Oxford University Press, 1999.

Darsow, Julie Barkl and Verlene Makalous Jackson. *Tornado Tales : Of Fear, Faith, and Courage*. Chapman, KS: ReVeal Publishing, 2009.

Fitzgerald, Daniel C. *Sound and Fury: A History of Kansas Tornadoes, 1854–2008*. Palm Harbor, FL: self-published, 2008–2009.

Flora, Snowden D. *Tornadoes of the United States*. Norman, OK: University of Oklahoma Press, 1953.

Grazulis, Thomas P. *The Tornado: Nature's Ultimate Windstorm*. Norman, OK: University of Oklahoma Press, 2001.

Hamric, Sharon and the staff of *The Wichita Eagle*. *Like the Devil: The Kansas Tornadoes of April 26, 1991*. Wichita: The Wichita Eagle and Beacon Publishing Co., 1991.

Haney, Janice, ed. *Greensburg: The Twisted Tales*. Greensburg, KS: self-published, 2008.

Marsh, Richard, ed. *The Day the Sky Fell: A picture report of the Topeka Tornado, June 8, 1966*. Topeka: *Topeka Capital-Journal*, 1966.

Menninger, Bonar. *And Hell Followed With It: Life and Death in a Kansas Tornado*. Austin, TX: Emerald Book Company, 2011.

Smith, Michael. *Warnings: The True Story of How Science Tamed the Weather*. Austin, TX: Greenleaf Book Group Press, 2010.

US National Oceanic and Atmospheric Administration. *Tornado*. Washington, DC: US Department of Commerce, National Oceanic and Atmospheric Administration, 1976.

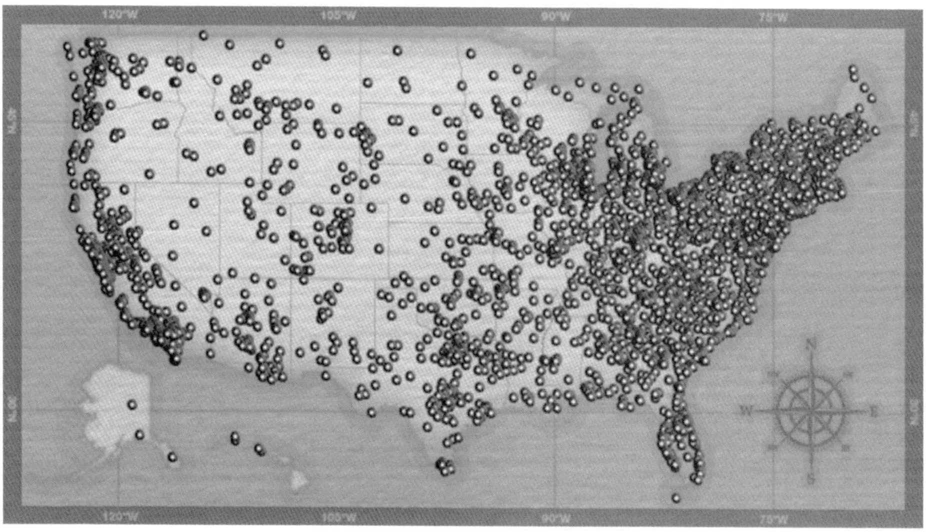